PROPHETIC JOURNEY

THE GOD OF YOUR TIGHT PLACES

PASTOR JOEY ZAMORA

aBM

Published by:
A Book's Mind
PO Box 272847
Fort Collins, CO 80527

Copyright © 2019
ISBN: 978-1-949563-73-3
Printed in the United States of America

ACKNOWLEDGEMENTS

Thank you, Meredith, for believing in me and supporting me. I'm so thankful that I have you to walk through all of our tight places together.

Thank you to Raquel & Aaron, Joey & Karli, Levi, and JP for giving me purpose. Avery and Amelia, you are my legacy and I wrote this book for you.

Thank you, Doug and Donna, for inspiring me to write. Your patience and generosity have made this project possible.

Thank you, Aaron, for lending your design skills and creativity to this project. You are brilliant!

ENDORSEMENTS

Life is a journey and every person will experience a tight season and a tight place. It takes prophetic insight to know how to navigate it properly and to come out of it better than when you went into it. It takes a special prophetic mantle to help others see pregnant potential in tight places. Joey Zamora is uniquely called and gifted to do just that. *Prophetic Journey* is something I would recommend to everyone.

Bishop Michael Pitts
Founder, Cornerstone Global Network

The journey from a dream to reality, from potential to promise, can be confusing and daunting. Yet, there is something deep inside the soul that continues to yearn for more. In this book, my friend Joey Zamora becomes a tour guide for the person who is on the pathway to pursuing purpose. His prophetic analysis of how biblical characters overcame difficult seasons and still arrived at their divine destination provides a roadmap on how you can do the same. As you read this book, you will receive wisdom and seasoned insight on how to voyage into a future of freedom and fulfillment. Get this book and start your journey today!

Jeffrey S. Smith
Lead Pastor, Strong Tower
President, JSS Consulting, Inc.

Prophetic Journey is a wonderful picture of God's presence in the midst of our trying times. Pastor Joey Zamora describes how God is with us not only in our highs, but He's also there in our lows. We are assured that as God walked with the patriarchs, He is with us, too. Our devastation isn't the end, it leads to our dominion!

Robert Sanchez
Prophet Rob Sanchez Ministries

FORWARD

The following pages of this book will take you on a journey that you might recognize not just in the lives of the men and women we celebrate week after week in our sermons and teachings, but also in your own life. Almost 30 years ago, Joey and I got married and shortly after started out in ministry and I could never have imagined the wild journey our life would become. I can't say it's all been easy, but I can say that God has brought us through every trial and hardship. We have learned so much along the way! Sometimes the lessons have been effortless and other times they have left us with lasting wisdom on how not to do or handle certain things – not unlike the patriarchs you will study.

I am so proud of my husband as he has poured his heart into this book, gleaning not only from the revelation God has blessed him with but the wisdom we have learned. It is my privilege to write this forward, but more than that to share this journey with Joey and now with you. This book will help you and ultimately encourage you as you navigate life with all of its ups and downs, wide open spaces, and tight and constricted areas. Just know that whenever you find yourself in a tight place, and from time to time you probably will, that God is the God of those places in your life also. He never has and He never will leave you or forsake you.

So, just like the conversation a stewardess might have with you before a plane takes off, let me tell you now – go ahead a put your seat in the upright position, make sure your seatbelt is buckled, and sit back and enjoy the ride. We've got places to go!

Meredith Zamora
Pastor, Cornerstone Church Tri-Cities

INTRODUCTION

"An evil man is ensnared by the transgression of his lips,
but the righteous escapes trouble."
Proverbs 12:13 (ESV)

On an early flight on a Monday morning in the first week of October a few years ago, my wife and I were coming home from a long week of ministry in Toledo, Ohio. As I looked out the airplane window shortly after take-off, I began to ponder all the lives that were changed and challenged that whole week. As I continued to gaze out the window, I was thanking God for the upgrade to first class (being 6'3" and 250 pounds, I was especially grateful!). I kept telling myself that I better get some sleep because it had been a long week of meetings and I had been up most of the night with my pastor, Bishop Michael Pitts, talking about the conference that had just taken place. But, it was one of those moments when I could sense that God wanted to speak to me. When that happens, I usually stay very still, but this time I scrolled through my Bible to the book of Proverbs and I read to chapter 12. When I got to verse 13, I read it over and over and over again.

I began to meditate on that verse and then went to my Strong's Concordance to look up every word of the text. When I got to the word "trouble," I discovered that it means "tightness,"[1] and for the next few hours, the Lord uncovered His Word to me and downloaded this book while I was still 30,000 feet in the air!

When I saw all the times this word was mentioned, I could see that God is the God of all of our tight and troubled places. As I dove into the Word, I began to see that every great patriarch and matriarch of the faith had similar

---

1   Strong, James. "Trouble," Hebrew 6869. *Strong's Exhaustive Concordance of the Bible.* Iowa Falls, Iowa: World Bible Publishers, 1986.

stories, where God would give them a word or a dream or a vision, where they would be excited, and then the process began to bring the development for their intended purpose.

As I began to research, I was able to see and understand a little bit more about how God works. I have pastored for almost 20 years now, and I have seen people, friends, and colleagues give in and give up because the process was too hard. All of us who are called by God to do something for our generation will go through difficult times, just like the patriarchs of old. But, the same God Who delivered them out of their tight and troubled places is the same today, yesterday, and forever (see Hebrews 13:8)! We know from Romans 2:11 that He is no respecter of persons. If He saw Moses through the Red Sea, He will see you through dark and dreadful times, and if He saw Daniel through the lion's den, He will see you through any crazy tight place. God is the only One Who stands the test of time.

My intention in writing this book is to encourage anyone who feels alone, distressed, or even afraid of the unknown. I can relate to wanting to give up and throw in the towel to surrender! But, quitting is not an option! Ecclesiastes 3 lists every time and every season – 28 of them, in fact – but, my friends, there is never a time to give up! I write this to you with godly conviction to inspire you to get up, shake yourself off, and get back in the game because God is the God of our tight places!

When I was in the third grade, I was the checkers champion in my class. My teacher was the three-time defending champion, and I beat her to become class champion. How did I do it, you may ask. Well, I beat her because I had one more checker than she did that had gone to the other side – and we all know that when a checker crosses the other side, you say, "King me!" That's when checkers that were jumped over and put out of the game now can come back into the game, and they become twice as powerful because now they can move forward *and* backward. I have a deep sense that God is saying, "KING ME!" You might have been out of the game for a while and you might have been in some tight situations, but you are coming back in the game with twice the power! God will give you power to dream. He will show you the power of His grace so that you will have the power to forgive and experience increase, blessing, and unity in your life again. I am persuaded that God's faithfulness will lead you and guide you through your prophetic journey and will deliver you from all of your tight places.

CHAPTER 1

THE POWER OF A DREAM
FROM A TIGHT PLACE TO A DOMINION PLACE

I'm going to begin with Joseph's prophetic journey – from his dream to his devastation to his development, all the way to his dominion. As we embark on our survey of the life of this great patriarch, I want to inspire and awaken the dreamer inside of you. As we will see, his journey of ups and downs and ins and outs was all part of God's purpose of working all things together for good. I feel that this story has the content to charge you, challenge you, and hopefully, change you as hidden truths from Joseph's life are revealed. I pray that the spirit of wisdom and revelation in the knowledge of Jesus Christ be present as you journey with me and experience the power to dream, and that it will take you, just like Joseph, from a tight place to a dominion place.

Let me first lay a foundation of some primary principles that connect to the events we will then explore in the life of Joseph.

LET NO MAN STEAL YOUR CROWN

Revelation 3:11 says, *"Behold, I am coming quickly! Hold fast what you have, that no one may take your crown."* This Scripture was written to the church in Philadelphia, the church of brotherly love. This church was given the key of David, that would open doors no man could shut and shut doors no man could open. This is a powerful promise to the church that understands love. In verse 8, Jesus begins to tell them that He has set an open door for them and that no man can shut it because they have kept His Word and have not denied His name. Verse 10 goes on to say that because they kept the word of patience, He would keep them from the hour of temptation. That leads into what we read in verse 11.

When we keep God's Word in whatever form it comes and don't deny His name, we, too, will have the key of David, which is the key of love and forgiveness that will open up doors nobody can close. God has set an open door before us (see verse 8), and all we have to do is walk, run, jump through it, and possess our promise in our dominion!

KEEPING HIS WORD

The Greek word for "kept" means "to guard, to protect, to do,"[2] so the church of Philadelphia received the key of David because they guarded, protected, did His Word, and never denied His Name. There are important principles to be learned here in this text. If we hold fast to His word, there will be all kinds of benefits. We know, for example, that His Word is a lamp unto our feet and a light unto our path (see Psalm 119:105); His Word is a battle axe and weapon of war (see Jeremiah 51:20); and, His Word is sharper than a two-edged sword (see Hebrews 4:12). Isaiah 55:11 tells us that His word does not return to Him void or empty, but it accomplishes what it was sent out to do!

Keeping God's Word is keeping His covenant. He is a covenant-keeping God. All the trouble that Israel, the patriarchs, or other familiar Bible figures had came when they did not believe God at His Word. God loves to be trusted with His Word, which is why James 1:22 tells us that we have to not just be hearers, but doers of the Word. If you never receive His Word, you can never believe His Word. If you never believe His Word, you can never become His Word. If you never become His Word, you can never do His Word. If you never do His Word, you can never give His Word. That's why God loves it when you keep, guard, hear, do, and give His Word – it brings you to open doors of great possibilities.

THE POWER OF HIS NAME

My wife and I got married on July 20, 1991. After we exchanged vows, she took my name, and the moment she did that, she had access to everything that

---

2   Strong, James. "Kept," Greek 5432. *Strong's Exhaustive Concordance of the Bible.* Iowa Falls, Iowa: World Bible Publishers, 1986.

belongs to me, from my money, to my car, and yes, even my bass boat! Up until that incredible day, she didn't have legal access to any of it. Philippians 2:9-10 says that, *"Jesus has been given the name above every name, that at the name of Jesus, every knee should bow, of things in Heaven, and things in earth, and things under the earth; and that every tongue should confess that Jesus Christ is Lord, to the glory of God the Father."* The name of Jesus is the most powerful name in the universe and He has given His name to everyone who is born again! Wow! Think about it. The name above all names is given to everyone who believes. That's incredible!

In Exodus 20:24, God makes a promise to His people that wherever His name is honored in worship, He would be there and bless them. A blessing at the end of a service denotes that the service has come to an end. We call that a benediction. When you honor the name of Jesus in your time of worship, He shows up and releases His benediction or His blessing, declaring that He will be faithful to finish what He started in your life._

THE OPEN DOOR

What is the open door? To the believer, the open door is Jesus. John 10:7 says that Jesus is the "door of the sheep." At the cross, Jesus became that open door. For a door to open correctly, it first has to be hung. So, Jesus was hung at the cross, and now He has become the open door of righteousness, according to Psalm 118:19. In verse 20, it goes on to say, *"This door of the Lord, into which the righteous shall enter."* Jesus is the open door through which we enter into our blessings, our protection, and our dominion. As Acts 17:28 says, *"In Him, we live and move and have our being."*

Psalms 118:22-24 says, *"The stone which the builder's refused is become the head stone of the corner. This is the Lord's doing; it is marvelous in our eyes. This is the day which the Lord hath made; we will rejoice and be glad in it."* So, the day the Lord made for us was the day that Jesus died on the cross for us all and rose from the dead and ascended to the right hand of the Father. Jesus is that open door into the glory of God!

THE DREAM

Moving on now to the life of Joseph, we see the hand of God, the faithfulness of God, and the perseverance of a man with his dream, even through intense devastation.

> *"Now Israel loved Joseph more than all his children, because he was the son of his old age. Also he made him a tunic of many colors. But when his brothers saw that their father loved him more than all his brothers, they hated him and could not speak peaceably to him. Now Joseph had a dream, and he told it to his brothers; and they hated him even more. So he said to them, 'Please hear this dream which I have dreamed: There we were, binding sheaves in the field. Then behold, my sheaf arose and also stood upright; and indeed your sheaves stood all around and bowed down to my sheaf.' And his brothers said to him, 'Shall you indeed reign over us? Or shall you indeed have dominion over us?' So they hated him even more for his dreams and for his words. Then he dreamed still another dream and told it to his brothers, and said, 'Look, I have dreamed another dream. And this time, the sun, the moon, and the eleven stars bowed down to me.' So he told it to his father and his brothers; and his father rebuked him and said to him, 'What is this dream that you have dreamed? Shall your mother and I and your brothers indeed come to bow down to the earth before you?' And his brothers envied him, but his father kept the matter in mind."*

Genesis 37:3-11

I am amazed at the faithfulness of a loving God who is willing to give a dream to Joseph, a 17-year-old, that will help him as he gets thrust into his prophetic journey, and that will move him from a tight place to a dominion place of ruling and reigning. This dream that God gives Joseph will become the rope of hope to all of his distresses along the way, strengthening him and motivating him when times get tough.

DREAM KILLERS

It seems as though when God gives someone a word of prophecy or a dream, the enemy begins to work against that dream or word right away by assigning what I call "dream killers" of our prophetic journey. We also could say that Joseph may have invited the mistreatment by telling his dreams to his half-brothers, which stirred up envy, strife, and animosity towards him. I do believe you should be careful who you tell your dream to, but in the end, it is still God Who works all things together for the good to them who love Him and are called according to His purpose (see Romans 8:28).

Whether or not you tell people your dream, you will have dream killers assigned to kill it – and, sometimes, they are very close to you or even related to you! In Matthew 16:21-23, when Jesus was telling His disciples that He was going to the cross to die for the whole world, Peter started to rebuke Jesus and said this would not happen! Jesus then told Peter, *"Get thee behind Me, Satan; you are an offense unto Me."* Sometimes, the people closest to us have the potential to be our greatest "satans."

My parents pastored a church for ten years and I was their Associate Pastor. From time to time, guest ministries would come and bless our church. It seemed that every prophetic voice that came in would see the prophetic call on my wife and I, and they would prophesy that it was time for the changing of the guards and time to pass the baton. But, my parents were having a hard time releasing their "baby" to us, feeling as though we were too young. This went on for a few years until my parents realized that they were hindering us. Having done ministry now for more than 20 years, I can honestly say that most of the hindrances we have encountered are with people who are close to us.

But, know that dream killers are needed. Those who despise or do not recognize or understand the call of God on your life are the ones God will use like a pawn in His hand. Jesus was betrayed and denied by His very own disciples, those He was close with, and we see the same pattern in Joseph's prophetic journey. God is able to make all grace abound toward you, no matter the situation. It was God Who used Joseph's brothers to get him where He needed him!

THE DEVASTATION

Joseph was the son of Rachel, the wife of Jacob, for whom Jacob worked for 14 years. Rachel was the woman of Jacob's dreams and the love of his life. Rachel was barren until one day God opened her womb and she conceived Joseph, her firstborn son. As we saw above, the Bible says that, *"Israel loved Joseph more than all of his children, because he was the son of his old age."* Israel gave Joseph a coat of many colors. This signified firstborn status, causing much jealousy and hatred toward Joseph. It seemed that, from that moment on, Joseph was at a disadvantage as it related to his brothers. So, when Joseph received the two dreams about ruling over his family and told them, it's no wonder they became outraged! The dream caused his brothers to hate him even more. Joseph became known to them as "the dreamer."

One day, according to the remainder of Chapter 37, his father told him to go check on the brothers, and his prophetic journey began. As Joseph was journeying along, he ran into a man who knew where they were, and as he approached them in his coat of many colors, his brothers remarked, "Look, the dreamer comes." They said amongst themselves, "Let's kill him and throw him in a pit," and his oldest brother Rueben said not to kill him, but to just throw him into a pit (that way he could deliver him back to his father later.) But, his brothers stripped him of his coat and threw him in. I can't imagine what was going through Joseph's head. One moment, he was on top of the world, and the next moment, he was in a pit with no coat, totally devastated.

Sometimes, we don't understand the stripping that takes place in our lives, but thanks be to God Who knows our end from our beginning. God had so much more for Joseph than just to rule over his father's house, so He allowed it.

Continuing in Joseph's story (verses 25-36), as the brothers sat to eat bread, they saw a company of Ishmaelites coming from Gilead and sold Joseph to them. When they arrived in Egypt, this group then sold Joseph to Potiphar, a well-known man. Let me interject a powerful truth right here. Ishmael was a son produced from Abraham's loins and Sarah's head (mind). Sarah couldn't have children, and they were trying to bring God's word to pass their own way. While the circumstances that brought about Ishmael's birth are typically thought of as a big mistake, it's still amazing to me that God can use our mistakes to bring deliverance years later. Our past mistakes, as desperate as they may have been, could someday deliver someone in desperate need.

Continuing with the story, God was with Joseph, and it seemed that no matter where Joseph ended up, the favor of the Lord would promote him time and time again. Joseph became very useful to Potiphar, so he promoted Joseph by giving him another coat, this time to rule over Potiphar's house and business affairs. Shortly afterwards, Potiphar's wife started noticing Joseph and propositioned him. Joseph denied her advances and she falsely accused him to Potiphar, who put him in prison (see Genesis 39). So, Joseph found himself in prison, stripped of two coats now! But, even after being sold by his brothers and falsely accused by Potiphar's wife, he still held onto his dream.

We can learn a great deal from Joseph's tenacity in keeping God's Word and not denying His name. Joseph held onto that dream through every step of his journey. When you are going through devastating times, you need to let the Word of God become the anchor with the rope of hope tied to it. Be encouraged, my friend. No weapon formed against you can prosper, as we see in Isaiah 54:17. If God spoke to you in a dream or a prophecy, He will bring it to pass!

As long as you hold onto the dream and do not allow the dream killers to kill it, God will see to it that you get promoted everywhere you go – even if that means the prison! Genesis 39:21 records, *"But the Lord was with Joseph, and showed him mercy, and gave him favor in the sight of the keeper of the prison."* Remember that God works all things after the counsel of His will (see Ephesians 1:11) and He also knows your end from your beginning. All your devastation can become the development for your intended purpose.

THE DEVELOPMENT

Proverbs 18:16 says, *"A man's gift makes room for him, and brings him before great men."* I have seen this verse come to pass in my own life, as my prophetic gift has brought me to know great people and be on great platforms. I see it no differently in Joseph's case. He still developed and operated in his gift at every stage of his journey and it brought him into places and platforms of influence. The development is a process of unfolding capabilities and possibilities in a person's life.

We must take God's Word and keep it and guard it, not denying His name, for in it is the remedy through our devastation and development. As with Joseph, God takes the good, the bad, and the ugly and works it all together for our good. One day we can feel as though we are on top of the world and the next day we can feel down in the dumps. One moment we're in, the next moment we're out. Our development leads us from faith to faith, from strength to strength, and from glory to glory if we can yield to the motion of our Creator. By submitting to His hand of development as it produces every zig and every zag in our life, He is faithful to make all our crooked places straight and all of our rough places smooth, preparing us to rule and to reign. Let no one steal the crown God has crafted for you!

As Joseph continued being faithful to God's dream, and at times holding on for dear life, he realized that what God had said would prove to be just as He said it would be. We see the faithfulness of a loving God toward His servant Joseph. Genesis 40 reads that one day, the King of Egypt got offended with his butler and baker and put them both in prison, where Joseph got to serve them. They both dreamed dreams and needed someone to interpret them. Joseph said, in verse 8, *"Do not interpretations belong to God? Tell them to me."* The two dreams, though seemingly different, were the same dream. They were about three days and a hanging. I know what you are thinking – that sounds like Jesus, when He said in John 2:19, *"Destroy this temple and in three days I will raise it up."* It's amazing to me that with all that Joseph had been through, he was still sensitive enough to interpret the dreams. The dreams were about three days and a hanging, where one man must die that another man may live. The dreams show us a type of resurrection power and redemption of position. Joseph was in a low place, the prison, but he still managed to allow his gift to operate. This shows his devotion to God and God's devotion to Joseph's development.

What I love about this redemptive story is that as Joseph was hearing and interpreting the dreams, he was not realizing that that dream is a dream about his development. Yes, the dream was about the butler and the baker and, yes, the baker dies and the butler lives, but there are so many parallels here. Jesus is the bread of heaven who died for the sins of the world so that He would be raised up as a new creation to be our heavenly "butler," to give us the drink offering of new wine, the Holy Spirit, so that we can be empowered from on high to live a Christian life here on earth. What Joseph is not realizing is that when God gives anyone a dream, that dream goes through a process of development for death, so at the end only God can raise what's dead.

Joseph received two dreams. The first dream was about the sheaves bowing down to his sheaf. The other dream was about the sun, the moon, and the stars bowing to him. The first dream was earthly and the second was heavenly. There is a principle in Hebrews 10:9 that states *"He takes away the first, that He may establish the second."* That's why the first Adam could not redeem humanity, but the second Adam could. That's why Ishmael, who was a product of flesh, Abrahams loins and Sarah's head, could not obtain the promise, but Isaac could because he was the son of promise or the second son. This is why God hated Esau, but loved Jacob. Jacob is the second son, but he receives the promise and the inheritance. This is why with our first birth, it is commanded for everyone to die once, but with our second birth, we are destined to live forever. That's why we are to be born again!

Joseph is not only interpreting for the butler and the baker, he is really interpreting the development of his own dream. In essence, one dream must die so that the other dream may live. It's no different from when Jesus died on the cross. When Jesus died on the cross, He died for all mankind. He said, according to John 12:32, *"If I be lifted up, I will draw all men to myself,"* signifying how He would die. When Jesus died, we all died to that old man and old nature, but when He rose from the dead, we all rose up as God's new creation in the earth. When Joseph was speaking life to the butler and death to the baker, he was in essence speaking life to his heavenly dream and death to his earthly dream.

What I love about Joseph is that he used his devastation for development. When the butler got restored, Joseph had one request: Remember me! Just like the thieves who hung on the cross next to Jesus (see Luke 23:39-42)! One said, "If you are the Christ, then save yourself," and the second thief said, "Please remember me when you get into paradise." And Jesus replied, "Today, you will be with me in paradise." With Jesus, it's always today! Even though the butler forgot about Joseph, it was only for a season of two full years. When Pharaoh had a dream that no one could interpret, it was the butler who remembered

Joseph. When he got called up to the palace, it was the beginning of his dream of ruling and reigning in his dominion unfolding.

THE DOMINION

When Pharaoh called for Joseph, the time and season had come for him to do what he was faithful in doing when things were good and when things were bad. Joseph had passed test after test with flying colors. With his devotion intact, the Word of God dear to his heart, and the name of his God on his lips, he would be strengthened in his inner man, knowing that his God would promote and bless him in due time. If you find yourself in a difficult season, be encouraged by this great patriarch! Put your trust in God's Word, never deny His beautiful name, and watch things turn around for you and your whole house.

In Genesis 41, Joseph was presented to the King in the palace. He had to wash, shave, and change garments. There was a removing of the old and a changing into the new so that he would be presentable to the King. As Pharaoh proceeded to tell Joseph the dreams he had, God gave Joseph the wisdom to interpret them. Because Joseph was faithful to interpret the dream of the butler and the baker in the lowest of lows, the prison, God gave Joseph the opportunity to interpret in the highest of highs, the palace. After Joseph interpreted the dream, he was put in charge, second only to the King.

It's amazing when you stay faithful to the dream God gives you, regardless of its ups and downs. Joseph had been through some tough times, but went from being in the lowest of places to as high as ruling and reigning in the King's palace – simply because he interpreted a dream! God put him back in position to have dominion. He went from being stripped of the coat of many colors and stripped of Potiphar's coat to ruling and receiving a robe, a ring, a golden chain, and the second chariot of Pharaoh. Only God can do that!

What does Ephesians 3:20 say? God is able to do exceedingly, abundantly above what you can ask or think! So, beloved, I exhort you to not lose heart in the middle of your ups and downs, for He Who called you is faithful to perform His Word over your life. If He did it for Joseph, He can do it for you. When God gives you a dream, beware of the dream killers who are only out to destroy what God has put in you. Know that when God gives you a dream, there will always be times of devastation, disappointment, and distress, but God will allow you to develop your gift in the middle of hard and difficult times. Stay faithful to your development and growth as a believer in the God you serve, for He is faithful to see you through to your place of dominion where you can fulfill your God-given dream to rule and reign.

I believe that understanding the dream, the devastation, the development, and the dominion will help you navigate your prophetic journey, and move you from a tight place to a dominion place.

In the next chapter, we will be moving from a tight place into a grace place. Let's continue our journey together.

CHAPTER 1 – POWER POINTS

- Keeping and guarding God's Word will bring you the key of David, opening doors no one can shut and shutting doors no one can open!
- Jesus has given us the power and authority to operate in His name.
- Our dream may bring devastation, but it's all part of the development needed to bring us into a place of dominion.

CHAPTER 2

THE POWER OF GRACE
FROM A TIGHT PLACE TO A GRACE PLACE

I want to cover transitioning from a tight place to what I'd like to call a "grace place." We learned in the introduction that, according to Proverbs 12:13, God delivers the just from all their trouble or, as we're calling it, all their tight places. I believe this shows us that if we are just and righteous, God is faithful to deliver us. As we will see in several other scenarios from both the Old Testament and the life of Jesus, God desires to not only deliver us, but to bring us into a revelation of His grace.

Let's learn more about this grace place. This place called grace is a place of God's unmerited favor, providence, intervention, and truth. In fact God's grace is so high you can't get over it, so low you can't get under it, and so wide you can't get around it. You can't work for it, be good enough for it, or earn it, buy it, or win it. All you have to do is receive it. It's simply a place where God's love unfolds on your behalf and enables and empowers you to do what you could not do for yourself. It is also a place of your identity as a son or daughter of God that gives you access to your inheritance. God's grace pulls back the veil of limitation and reveals the truth of His righteousness in the believer's life.

Hannah's Grace Place

In 1 Samuel 1, we find the account of Elkanah and his wives, Penninah and Hannah. We know from the story that Penninah had children, but Hannah was barren. The first point I want to make here is from verse 5, where it says that every year, Elkanah would go up to the city to worship and sacrifice to the Lord. He would give portions to Penninah and her children, but to Hannah, he gave a double portion. (It's not the focal point of this chapter, but I believe this shows us that God wants to give us double for our trouble – double for our tight places!) It goes on to say that the Lord had closed Hannah's womb and her rival, Penninah, provoked her severely and it made her miserable, to the point that she wept and did not eat. Elkanah tried to comfort her, but it says she was in bitterness of soul and prayed to the Lord and wept in anguish (see verse 10).

THE VOW

Let's focus in on what she did next. Verse 11 tells us that Hannah made a vow, promising the Lord that if He looked on her affliction, remembered her, and gave her a son, she would return him to the Lord all the days of his life and a razor would never touch his head. Eli, the high priest, said to her, "Go in peace and may the God of Israel grant your petition which you have asked of him" (see verse 17). In the next verse, she replied to him, "Let your maidservant find grace in your sight." Then, Hannah went on her way and she ate and her countenance was no longer sad. This portion of the story concludes in verses 19-20 by telling us that they rose early in the morning and they worshiped before the Lord. Then, they returned and came to the house of Ramah and it came to pass in the process of time that Hannah conceived and bore a son named Samuel saying, "because I have asked for him from the Lord."

THE CLEANSING

Hannah's name means "grace," but the reality of her condition blinded her to see her true character and nature until she rose up from the peace offering meal and went to the temple of God and wept, which is a type of cleansing, forgiveness, and repentance. Her weeping, in fact, was mistaken by the high priest Eli as drunkenness. She was not drunk, as Eli supposed, just hungry spiritually to see her heart's desire come to pass.

When Eli saw that she was not drunk, he knew she was desperately praying for her breakthrough. So, in verse 17, Eli replied to Hannah, "Go in peace: and the God of Israel grant you thy petition that you have asked of him." Hannah, in verse 18, says, "Let your handmaid find grace in your sight." Hannah ("grace") did not discover herself until she found her grace place in the temple of God, in the eyes of the high priest. In other words, she discovered her identity as a daughter of God, and she received her inheritance and promise. Then and only then could she recover what she discovered in the eyes of the high priest, which was the grace to receive and the grace to conceive the son of promise for which she had prayed and believed.

THE HOUSE OF BREAD

We see another story in the book of Ruth, where a man by the name of Elimel-ech and his wife Naomi had two sons, Mahlon and Chilion. They were from Bethlehem Judah, which means "house of bread and blessing." In the first chapter, we see that they had moved to the land of Moab, away from this bread and blessing. Their two sons took wives from the land of Moab. Mahlon married Orpah and Chilion married Ruth. After about ten years of living there, Elimelech died. Shortly after that, Mahlon and Chilion also died, leaving only the woman. Naomi had gotten word that the Lord had visited her people in Bethlehem Judah by giving them bread. So, according to verses 8-10, she rose up, gathered her two daughters-in-law, and said, "Go, return each to her mother's house: the Lord deal kindly with you, as you have dealt with the dead and with me." Then, she kissed them and they lifted up their voices and wept. Further in that chapter, we see Ruth's insistence on staying with Naomi.

> "And Ruth said, 'Intreat me not to leave thee, or to return from fol-lowing after thee: for whither thou goest, I will go; and where thou lodgest, I will lodge: thy people shall be my people, and thy God my God: where thou diest will I die, and there will I be buried: the Lord do so to me, and more also, if ought but death part thee and me.'"
>
> Ruth 1:16-17

This story is interesting to me because there is so much prophetic insight to this. Let me start by saying that John 1:17 shows us that grace is connected to truth. Truth was discovered in Bethlehem Judah, the place of provision and substance, the house of bread and praise and worship, which symbolizes truth. The moment that Naomi, who represents grace, departs from the place of truth, it seems as though everything starts falling apart, and in the tenth year, things begin to die. The number 10 is symbolic of the Law, and where the Law is, there is sin and death, according to Romans 8:2. The moment when Naomi discovers that there is bread in Bethlehem Judah (speaking of the Word of God, which is truth), we see that there is a plan of recovery. When grace (Naomi) and truth (Bethlehem Judah) find a common place to dwell together, then, and only then, do we find a true recovery of what has been lost. Bethlehem Judah was the place where grace and truth could dwell together to bring a recovery to the blessing.

God is the God of restoration and He does that by His great grace that He provides for us all. Anytime grace and truth kiss, the power of His blessing begins to manifest. We know as soon as Naomi and Ruth returned from their journey from Moab to Bethlehem Judah, the place of God's truth, the blessing of God began to manifest on behalf of this great family's obedience. We see tremendous favor released upon Ruth to glean in Boaz's field. There, she would be recognized by Boaz himself and find favor in his eyes, and he would promote her to glean from the best of the field and eventually marry him and own the field. You see, when grace and truth come together, the blessing can't help but manifest on your behalf. Just like Ruth, when you attach yourself to grace and truth, it leads you straight into the blessing God has always intended for you.

GRACE AND TRUTH TO BE CLEAN

Another similar story that shows us this connection between grace and truth is found in 2 Kings 5, where we see a man by the name of Naaman, who has leprosy. We find that Naaman is a captain of the Syrian army and is an honorable and well-respected man in Syria. The handmaid who tends to Naaman's wife is from Israel. In verse 3, she says to Naaman's wife, *"Oh, that my lord were with the prophet who is in Samaria! He would recover him of his leprosy."* Word got to the King of Syria, who in turn wrote a letter to the King of Israel. When the King of Israel read the letter, he tore his clothes and said, *"Am I God, to kill and make alive that this man does send me to recover a man of his leprosy?"* The king of Israel thought that the King of Syria was picking a fight with him, but it was set up by God. When Elisha heard about the situation, he told the King to send Naaman his way.

Before I go further with this, remember what I said earlier – the Law was given unto Moses, but grace and truth came by Jesus Christ. With that said, the name Naaman means "pleasant" or "grace" and it's actually the masculine form of "Naomi."[3] Naomi and Naaman mean the same thing. Jesus Christ came to bring grace *and* truth. Grace by itself will produce spiritual leprosy, which is flesh that is out of control. Grace needs truth because, according to Romans 5:21, grace reigns through righteousness. We have to do things right, or "in truth."

Naaman had to find his grace place so he could experience breakthrough and recovery. Elisha was God's prophet, who held the words of truth in his mouth. Naaman (grace) needed to find Elisha (truth) so that there could be recovery and healing in Naaman's life. Elisha told Naaman to go and dip in the Jordan River seven times. This shows us a grace place called the Jordan where grace takes a perfect dip (7 times) because of the word of truth, and that brings the manifestation of his recovery.

Both of these stories show people going through seasons of tight places only to discover their grace place in the middle of their dilemma. True recovery can only come from discovering your grace place, which is the place where grace and truth come together to reveal what is rightfully yours as a believer of Jesus Christ.

GRACE AND TRUTH TO SEE STRAIGHT

In Acts 9, Saul of Tarsus, who will eventually be called Paul the Apostle, is persecuting the church. Saul thinks he is fulfilling his God-given purpose as his zeal is spreading like wildfire because of his persecution toward the first-century church. But, as he approaches Damascus, he is confronted by Jesus, and we find this exchange:

"And he fell to the earth, and heard a voice saying unto him, Saul, Saul, why persecutest thou me? And he said, Who art thou, Lord? And the Lord said, I am Jesus whom thou persecutest: it is hard for thee to kick against the pricks."

Acts 9:4-5

---

3   Strong, James. "Naaman," Hebrew 5283. *Strong's Exhaustive Concordance of the Bible.* Iowa Falls, Iowa: World Bible Publishers, 1986.

The first thing I want you to notice is the correlation between Jesus and His Church. To the Lord, they are one and the same. If Jesus does not see a difference between Him and His Church, then we shouldn't either!

When Jesus confronted Saul, he fell to the ground, and he was blinded by Jesus's bright light. Saul was commanded to kill believing Christians because of the law. You see, my friends, the Law kills, but it is the Spirit that gives life, according to 2 Corinthians 3:6. Saul was blinded for three days until Jesus spoke to a certain disciple called Ananias in a vision, and said in Acts 9:11, *"Arise, and go into the street called Straight, and enquire in the house of Judas for one called Saul of Tarsus: for behold he prayeth, and has seen in a vision a man named Ananias coming in, and putting his hand on him that he might receive his sight."*

What I want you to see here is that Saul is blinded by the Light. He came to enforce the law or darkness. Jesus, on the other hand, is light. Light always exposes darkness and darkness does not comprehend it. Ananias's name means grace. Jesus spoke to a man whose name means grace and gave him the truth of His Word in a vision. Anytime you have grace and truth come together, it brings restoration and healing. God had a greater intention for Saul because the religious system wanted Saul for darkness, but Jesus wanted to transform Saul to Paul so that he could be a dispenser of light. Grace and truth are the only things that can open blind eyes, set the captive free, and make all the crooked ways straight. Just as grace and truth opened Saul's eyes, they will open up our eyes to see the hope of His calling for each and every one of us. We must discover our true identity by his grace and His truth through faith.

DISCOVERING YOUR TRUE IDENTITY

To understand the concept of identity, let's look at what happened when Jesus was baptized in the Jordan River. At that moment, He received His identity by His Father. God split the eastern skies and told everybody that this is His beloved Son in whom He is well pleased (see Matthew 3:17).

Let me give you some context on this. In the Jewish custom, a man was considered to have come into maturity at the age of 30. In the eyes of that custom, he didn't come into his full stature as a son until that time. This custom was called adoption – quite different from the kind of adoption we know here in the western world. This custom of adoption was when the father would place his boy as a son in his house. When he came forth out of the matrix of his mother, he was considered the son of his mother until he was bar mitzvahed, then he was considered the son of the law. One was considered the son of the law until the age of 30. At that time, his father would take him outside the city limits to where business was being conducted. He would introduce his son to his colleagues and clients, saying, "This is my son, and I am pleased with him. The words of his mouth from this point on are as good as if they had come from my mouth."

Now, keep in mind that at this point in history, God had not been speaking to the system of the Church. There were still altars and sacrifices, and occasionally we see that the waters were troubled here and there and so on (see John 5:4), but God had remained silent for over 400 years, not speaking to any priests. So, when Jesus was immersed in the waters of baptism and God spoke these words, we see the fresh significance of this moment based on the context of the Jewish culture. When God the Father began to speak of Jesus in this way, He was pronouncing that Jesus was authorized to do business on His behalf! He was saying that the voice of Jesus was the same as the voice of God and that the word in His mouth was as good as the word out of the mouth of God! Wow!

GOD'S APPROVAL

Watch what happens right after Jesus is baptized. It's this great moment, right? He gets confirmation of His identity from God the Father and you might think everything would be easy after this point. But, look at what happens at the beginning of Matthew 4. We see that after 40 days of fasting, Jesus is led into the wilderness to be tempted. Even more amazing is that it wasn't even the devil who led him in, it was the Holy Spirit! This shows us the principle that anything that God approves has to be proved. If God qualified Jesus as the Son of God, then Jesus had to be taken to the place of personal temptation.

The importance of understanding your true identity in Christ Jesus is so that you know what God has always known about you that you never knew about yourself. When you have an understanding that God is for you and not against you, and when you realize that "greater is He who is in you than He that is in the world" (see 1 John 4:4), it is the greatest significance you will ever come to know. That's when you realize the great grace of God. If you find yourself in a predicament or a trial or a temptation, you know that His grace is always sufficient to set free, deliver, and bring recovery to every aspect of your life.

If you find yourself in a tight place, know that the God you serve has a grace place awaiting you. A place full of grace and truth, a place of identity and inheritance.

A GARDEN PLACE

Building on this, let's look at Matthew 26:36-46, which recounts a crucial incident in the life of Jesus. We find him in the Garden of Gethsemane on the night before His crucifixion. The Garden represents that ugly, hateful, middle place between the place of identity and the place of grace. The Garden of Gethsemane was the pressing place, the place where Jesus endured the pressure. It represents not just the pressures you can see, but pressure you can feel. For us, it's the pressure we face every day – the pressure of marriage, children, our work, our church, our finances, our health, etc. It's the pressure of feeling stuck after fighting and fighting.

It's funny to me that Jesus went through this place of pressure in a garden. Gardens are supposed to be beautiful, right? Can I tell you that it's possible to be in a beautiful place and still encounter an ugly situation? Every day, we encounter unpleasant situations that arise in beautiful places. But, it is in those places that we discover what we're really made of. We discover how committed we really are. Those pressure situations force us to ask hard questions, even though we may feel like God is nowhere to be found. We know He is in us, but we can still feel like He's a million miles away. In those times of intense pressure, we stay connected, consistent, and committed because we know that still, somehow, when our sigh and our prayer ascend to God, as we learned from Hannah, He will cause a transformation from our tight place to a place of grace where He will enable and empower us.

THE PROCESS

Jesus was alone in the Garden of Gethsemane. Where were the multitudes He fed with the loaves and fishes? The ones who sat and listened to Him teach? What about the 70 people He commissioned? They were nowhere to be found. So, we find Jesus, who is Himself "the Alpha and the Omega," the beginning and the end, stuck in the ugly middle place. It was pressure time. In those times in our own lives, God is squeezing every ounce of oil, every ounce of fragrance out from the inside of us. God is the One working the situation. It is not the devil. It is not necessarily a popular place to be in, but God knows how much you can bear. He is there with you in your garden, but He wants to squeeze the oil out of you, and believe me when I say that He will squeeze you until you are sure you cannot be squeezed anymore!

He is a God Who is full of love, but He is the same God Who will cause you to endure the process. Why? Because every promise has a process and that process brings pain. If you have your eyes on the promise, you can use your pain to fuel yourself and your promise. Allow that oil that has been drawn out to be ignited by the God Who is an all-consuming fire!

Tight places are frustrating, without a doubt. It's frustrating to feel stuck, trapped, or disempowered. In fact, I have come to realize that when I am feeling frustrated, it is a sign that I am fed up and have out-grown my space and my place. But, understand that when you're feeling weary in well-doing or things feel tight and tough, there is a place of grace that God has prepared for you and the grace of God will shine the light to reveal the strength, courage, and ability you have on the inside of you. It will thrust you and promote you to higher places and spaces.

THE CONTRACTIONS

When my wife and I were getting ready to have a baby, we went to the hospital and they hooked her up to the monitor that tracks contractions. I thought it was pretty cool! As the contractions got stronger, after several hours, I started to announce to her, "Hey, you're having another contraction!" She would say, "I know I'm having another contraction!" It got to the point where my voice, out of all the voices in the room, became the most irritating and frustrating to her. Every time I announced another contraction, she would say, "Stop it! I *know*

I'm having a contraction! I can feel it! When you're seeing it, *I'm* feeling it. *We're* not having a baby, *I'm* having a baby!"

Let's compare this to what Jesus went through in the Garden of Gethsemane. He was feeling the contractions of Gethsemane, but there was no one there to identify with Him or go through that process with Him. He went off to meet with the Father and told the disciples to wait for Him, but when He came back, they were sleeping! Jesus went through the most difficult process of pressure as He prepared to fulfill His earthly purpose. You may think the battle of the cross was won at the cross. No, the battle of the cross was won in the garden. It was won in the tight place!

NEVERTHELESS

It is so tempting to look for help from others when we're in those tight places. In those places, we expect people to identify with us. We seek out and put our trust in and reliance on other folks. But, the problem is that those others don't have in them what we need for our tight place, our place of pressure. Even Jesus felt disappointed in that garden. God wasn't saying anything, and the disciples were sleeping. He was in a pressured place, sweating blood. This wasn't just anybody, this was Jesus, the Son of God, the Incarnate, and He was feeling the pressure!

Pay attention to what happens next. His words after all that despair were, *"Nevertheless, not my will, but Your will be done"* (see Matthew 26:39). Jesus was satisfied with what God had intended before the foundations of the world. He chose to endure what laid before Him.

This helps us see that people are the same everywhere you go, anywhere on the planet. Eventually, they're going to let you down and you must be willing and able to find your grace place, where you are okay with what God has intended for you to go through. God will empower you in that grace place. He will help you. He will turn your sigh into a song. He will take your trouble and make it pleasant. He will turn and shift things around for you.

FINDING YOUR GRACE PLACE

Places of praise, worship, prayer, and committed devotion allow you to lift your song and your sigh to the living God and He will enable you and help your through. This brings us back to the story we opened this chapter with, the story of Hannah. Remember that Hannah means "grace." Even though her name was grace, she was still barren, still unfruitful, and she still didn't understand the potential of God on the inside of her. She was loved by her husband, who was willing to give her double for her trouble, but she still had to deal with Penninah provoking her to jealousy, telling her what she couldn't do and couldn't produce. But, you know what? Penninah didn't know that her provocation was building character in Hannah, squeezing out any bitterness and anger.

This shows us that God wanted something from Hannah that only the irritation of Penninah could bring out of her. He's wanting something from us that only people can get out of us. Hannah was in the place where she was frustrated by all the ridicule and all the trouble. She was being provoked to bitterness. But, at some point, she saw herself getting up from that place. She found her grace place.

The anointing only comes when you have been through some tight places, some rough places, some sick places, and some hard places. When you've suffered so long and so successfully, God says, "I've removed bitterness out of you, I've removed anger out of you. Now, you really are a person who knows how to forgive, who knows how to operate in mercy." God puts us in situations that will draw out of us what we need. You need patience? He will allow you to be placed in situations that will work impatience out of you. There are secret places on the inside of you that are full of strength that you don't even know about, but they won't be released until you find a grace place. Hannah found hers when she prayed and poured out her heart before the Lord. God heard the song from her heart.

When I find myself in a tight place, I may still go through it tugging and pulling, feeling frustrated or even critical or judgmental. But, afterwards, I have so much more love for God, more insight into the Kingdom, and definitely more love for His people. Yes, I even had love for those people who, like the disciples, may have fallen asleep when I was looking for their support. You may not feel strong right now, but you'll find a grace place, a place of strength in God. The Bible, in Proverbs 18:10, tells us that *"The name of the Lord is a strong tower and the righteous run to it and are saved."* You will find that place in God where, even when people say there is no hope for you, you can say, like the psalmist in Psalm 3:3, "Yes, there is! The Lord is my shield, my glory, and the lifter of my head!"

GRACE TO STAND

When you realize you can stand, God will deliver you from your tight place to your grace place. When you learn to find your grace place, you will discover that God is faithful even when we're not. When we're tired, He's not. When we want to give up, He never gives up. God has built us with a grace to withstand. We will not collapse in the time of pressure! Find your grace place in the place of worship from a sincere heart and you'll discover that *that* atmosphere is where God redeems, restores, and reveals.

Though you are in the middle of tight places, troubled places, and pressure places, nobody ever has to know because there will be a certainty on the inside of you that God never built you to fail and He never built you to fall. He has hidden places on the inside of me and you that are yet to be tapped into and He will reveal those by His grace.

Look at the example of the Apostle Paul. Three times, he asked for the thorn in his side to be removed, but God didn't answer him until the fourth time, saying, *"My grace is sufficient for you"* (see 2 Corinthians 12). And, you know what? God's grace is sufficient for you, too. As you find your grace place, have faith for God to turn some things around in your life, lifting burdens and breaking yokes. I believe that you will see God in the midst of your tight place, and you'll find that He is ready to strengthen you by His grace, to respond to your sincere worship and the cry of your heart, to shift the situations you're facing, and to unlock potential on the inside of you.

Keep your head up! Discover your grace place and know that whatever you discover you have a right to recover! As we journey into the next chapter, my prayer is that the capacity of your heart will expand and that the Holy Spirit would reveal and convict with truth that would liberate. Now, let's explore moving from a tight place to a forgiving place.

CHAPTER 2 – POWER POINTS

- The tight place, the place of our trouble, has the potential to turn into our grace place.
- People will provoke us, disappoint us, or be unavailable when we need them, but it will force us to go after the heart of God, ultimately showing us that there is more inside of us than we realized.
- God responds to the sincerity of our heart's cry. The posture of praise and the atmosphere of worship create the potential for God's grace to manifest in our lives.

CHAPTER 3

THE POWER OF A PARDON
FROM A TIGHT PLACE TO A FORGIVING PLACE

We have seen what happened in the lives of Joseph, Hannah, and others when they found themselves in a tight place – how God showed Himself to be a deliverer, moving them from tight places to places of dominion and places of His grace. My goal in this chapter is to unveil the power of a pardon, moving you from a tight place to a forgiving place, by giving you insight into the life of King David.

THE POWER OF PARDON

I want to go now into the power of pardon, going from a tight place to a forgiving place. Jesus said it this way in Matthew 5:7, *"Blessed are the merciful, for they obtain mercy."* Mercy is just another word for forgiveness. Many of us have the opportunity to walk in unforgiveness, but Jesus is wanting us to walk guiltless before Him. He wants us to be free of any offenses that have come into our lives.

So, let's start in 1 Samuel 26:5-26. It recounts the story of David coming to the place where Saul had encamped. David went down with Abishai and they found Saul sleeping. Abishai said to David, "Today, God has delivered your enemy into your hand; now therefore, please let me strike him with the spear to the ground with one stroke, and I will not strike him the second time." But, David said to Abishai, "Do not destroy him, for who can stretch out his hand against the LORD'S anointed and be without guilt?" David went on to say, "The LORD forbid that I should stretch out my hand against the LORD'S anointed; but now please take the spear that is at his head and the jug of water, and let us go." David took the spear and the jug of water from beside Saul's head, and they left. When Saul realized what had happened, he said, "I have sinned. Return, my son David, for I will not harm you again because my life was precious in your sight this day." David replied, "The LORD will repay each man for his righteousness and his faithfulness; for the LORD delivered you into my hand today, but I refused to stretch out my hand against the LORD'S anointed. Now behold, as your life was highly valued in my sight this day, so may my life be highly valued in the sight of the LORD, and may He deliver me from all distress." Then Saul said to David, "Blessed are you, my son David; you will both accomplish much and surely prevail." The final verse tells us David went on his way and Saul returned to his place. We'll be building on this story as we move forward in this chapter.

When I was a kid, I heard Billy Graham tell a story of two friends who were walking through the desert. During some point of the journey, they had an argument and one friend slapped the other one right in the face. The one who got slapped got hurt, but without saying anything, he wrote in the sand, "Today, my best friend slapped me in the face." They kept on walking until they found an oasis where they decided to take a bath. The one who had been slapped got stuck and started to drown. But, the best friend saved him and after he recovered from the near drowning, he wrote on a stone, "Today, my best friend saved my life." The friend asked why he wrote the offense in the sand and the heroic deed on a stone, and he replied, "When someone hurts you, you should write it down in the sand where winds of forgiveness can erase it away. But, when someone does something good for you, you must engrave in the stone where no wind can never erase it." The moral of the story is that we must learn to write our hurts in the sand and carve our benefits in stone. Life is too short to waste time hating anyone! We should instead follow the words found in Philippians 4:8 and focus on things that are excellent and noteworthy.

We know that we do not war against flesh and blood but against principalities, rulers of the darkness, etc., right? We know that from Ephesians 6:12. However, I believe that even more than that, we struggle with the concept of occupation, which is possessing our promise and the inheritance that is in Christ Jesus. In Luke 19:13, Jesus is telling a parable where He says, *"Occupy until I come."* We as believers cannot sit and stay idle, doing nothing, when God has given us all things that pertain to life and godliness (see 2 Peter 1:3). We must put into action what we believe.

As a pastor, I stand before my congregation day in and day out, trying to teach and equip the body of Christ to really understand who God has created them to be. God told Moses that He was giving him a land that flowed with milk and with honey. We know that God gave it to him in that very moment, yet it still took 40 years for them to occupy the land! Additionally, Jesus Christ, through His death, burial, and resurrection, has given us all things that pertain to life and godliness (see 2 Peter 1:3), but it can take us a lifetime to understand what that really looks like!

THE DEVIL'S DEVICES

In 2 Corinthians 2:10, it says, *"Let us not be ignorant of the devil's devices."* That is referring to his schemes, perceptions, or the way he thinks. I believe one of the first steps in understanding how to occupy is to realize when we're in darkness and how to get out of it. In Jude 6, we read, *"The angels who did not keep their proper domain, but left their own abode, he has reserved."* There is a reservation or reserved place for the angels, for Satan, and for every member of the horde that came with him that fell from heaven when they left their domain. It says there is a place reserved in everlasting chains under darkness.

Darkness is the place of ignorance, of not knowing. The devil does not care what you believe! He wants you to stay ignorant, not knowing certain things, and to keep you "not knowing," because that's the place of his domain. The place of reservation that God gave to Satan to dwell is in the place of you "not knowing." He dwells in the place of darkness or the place where you don't know. It's the place of ignorance.

The prophet Hosea said that we are destroyed because of lack of knowledge (see Hosea 4:6). Light speaks of knowledge and understanding and darkness speaks of ignorance. This is why we have to understand that we can, according to Isaiah 60:1, arise and shine. Why? Because Jesus, the Light, has come! Knowledge and understanding have come! We do not have to be people of ignorance anymore.

Carrying this a step further, let's look at what happens when our eyes are opened to the power of forgiveness. Matthew 18 is a crucial portion of Scripture where Peter asks Jesus, *"Lord, how often shall my brother sin against me, and I forgive him? Up to seven times?"* Then Jesus replies in verse 22, *"I do not say to you, up to seven times, but up to seventy times seven."* That's 490 times! I can imagine Peter thinking, "What??"

The truth is that God is wanting us to forgive because, according to the familiar portion of The Beatitudes found in Matthew 5:7, *"Blessed are the merciful, for they shall obtain mercy."* Look, we have to sow mercy. We have to sow it because we are in need of mercy ourselves. We really are not as good and perfect as we think! Those who are not guilty need justice, but those who are guilty need mercy!

AMAZING GRACE

It's amazing that all of us as humans want to obtain the mercy of God, but when it comes down to the things or people in our own lives, we struggle with giving it. There is a classic hymn that everybody, including sinners, knows called "Amazing Grace." The song's lyrics say, "Amazing grace, how sweet the sound that saved a wretch like me, I once was lost, but now I am found; was blind, but now I see." We all want grace or mercy when it come to our shortcomings and failures, but I think this song should be sung like this: "Amazing grace, how sweet the sound that saved a wretch like you, you once were lost, but now are found, blind but now you see." The same grace or mercy that is good enough for me should be good enough for you!

We must show mercy because forgiveness is not for those who have hurt us – forgiveness is for us! It clears us out of the way, regardless of what offense happened. If we do not forgive, then it's easy for our thoughts to become consumed with the person who wronged us and every detail of the offense. It will eat us up every moment of every day! Pretty soon, we start imagining scenarios where we'd run into them… "Oh, if I see so-and-so, I'm going to say a thing or two. Yes, I am…" But, we must release them! I wouldn't be where I am today if I hadn't developed the ability to release. It is not easy, but it can be done!

It could be 490 times that you release that incident or that person or it could be 490 times in one day. It was a great revelation to me when I realized this process. I kept thinking, "Man, I thought I was over this…" Then, a month would go by and I'd find myself saying again, "Man, I thought I was over this." We can ask God to clear our hearts, but then we still have that little edge that won't smooth out, right?

I understand a little deeper now why Jesus said 490 times. In fact, the length of time from the book of Malachi to the book of Matthew was 400 years. God didn't speak to the system of the Church after the book of Malachi. They were "doing church," offering sacrifices and so on, but God was not in the system of the Church and He hadn't spoken to the Church. He would show up and trouble the waters every now and then, and He would show up as an angel and speak to certain things, but God Himself didn't open up His mouth until Jesus was immersed into the waters of baptism. That's when He said, "This is my Son, in whom I am well-pleased."

Now, let's fast-forward to the stoning of Stephen, recorded in Acts 7, after the death and resurrection of Jesus. Stephen was righteous – he didn't need mercy, he needed justice. And church people stoned him, not ordinary people! Church people wanted to stone a righteous man who had the power of God and they thought they were doing God's justice. This shows us a picture of the people we come across in life who throw stones at us, thinking they are doing God's justice. But, just as Stephen showed us, we still have to forgive them. Look at Stephen. He said, "Father, forgive them!" Jesus, at his death, said the same thing! He had done nothing wrong, but yet He had to look at the other side of the matter and say, according to Luke 23:34, *"Forgive them, for they know not what they do."* At that moment, God began to stand up from his throne. He sat on His throne for over 400 years, but we see in Acts 7:56, He stood up the day Stephen was stoned. It had been 490 years from the book of Malachi to the stoning of Steven! God stood up and said, in effect, "Okay, I'm done. I've got to deal with this now. I'm going to take the mantle that was on Stephen and I'm going to put it on Paul. You took one of my best, so I'm going to take, Church, one of your best." The Bible says that the mantle of Stephen fell at the foot of Saul of Tarsus. It was like God was saying, "I'm going to take him and he'll preach this gospel not to the Jews, but to the Gentiles!" Wow! Isn't that powerful?

So, now we have a deeper understanding of the reference to 490 times from Matthew 18. But, watch what happens immediately after that. Jesus goes on to speak with his disciples, telling them the parable of the unforgiving servant (see verse 23). In this parable, there was a king who wanted to settle accounts with his servants. When he began to settle, one servant was brought in who owed him 10,000 talents, but because he was unable to pay, his master commanded that he be sold, with his wife and children and all that he had, and that payment be made. That servant fell down before him, pleading for patience and promising to pay his debt in full. The master was moved with compassion, released him, and forgave his debt. Then, it goes on to say that this same servant went out and found one of his fellow servants who owed him a hundred denarii. This is like being pardoned millions of dollars and then finding someone who owes you maybe a hundred. It says the servant went out and found one his fellow servants who owed him a hundred denarii and he grabbed him by the neck, demanding that he pay back what he owed him. His fellow servant fell down at his feet and he begged him saying, "Have patience with me and I will pay you all." But, he would not listen! He actually threw him in prison until he could pay the debt! When his fellow servants saw what had been done, they were quite grieved and told their master all that had happened. The master then said to him, "You wicked servant! I forgave you all your debt because you begged me to. Should you not have also had compassion on your fellow servant just as I had pity on you?" His master was angered and handed him over to the jailers (the tormentors) until he could pay all that was due. Jesus went on to say in verse 35, *"So my heavenly Father will also do to you if each of you from his heart will not forgive his brother."*

I want to focus in on this because this is what builds us up and builds character in us. Each of us has to make the choice, regardless of how other people treat us, that the journey of life is also a journey of love. We have to shake off whatever tries to sway us to the left or to the right of what we know God has for us and be determined to look for the best in everything and everybody.

We simply have to be merciful. We have to, because we need mercy ourselves. We want God to deliver us out of our tight places, our troubled places.

We must find the mercy to say, "God, what they did to me was not necessarily right, but I know that I can forgive them because I'm able to forgive those who trespass against me. I know that You will deliver me from every tight situation, from a troubled narrow place, and from the place of frustration. I know that You are able to deliver me. I'm not going to stay in this darkness, this ignorant place, because I know too much now and I am able to release mercy and therefore obtain mercy."

This brings us back to my text from 1 Samuel 26. David, we see, had walked this journey called love. He knew what it was to be rejected, not just by people and not just by King Saul. It didn't start when he emerged to kingship, it started when he was a little kid when he was rejected by his own father and his own brothers. He's the one who would write the words in Psalm 118:22, *"The stone that the builders rejected. This one became the head of the corner…"* It was a prophetic revelation of the coming of Messiah, but it was David who had to live out that revelation. He was the stone that was rejected by his father and his brothers, the builders. Yet, he would find himself in a solitary place on the backside of the desert. There, he would find himself in the place of rejection with his harp. There, he would begin to cry out to the living God and there David would begin to write psalms. Just like we saw with Hannah, the sigh of his heart became his song. His rejection became his redemption. There, David learned to skillfully play the harp, and his skill brought him into the palace, to the presence of the king himself. When he was in the presence of a king, evil spirits would leave, simply by the way he played his instrument. Can you imagine what an anointing that was?

The backside of the desert is also where David practiced his swing and where he learned which stones to pick for his sling. I am positive that it wasn't the first time he had picked it up when he killed the giant Goliath. He had done it day in and day out! He must have practiced on anything that would run! David practiced in the middle of nowhere, when no one was watching him and no one was looking for him. David became skillful at everything he did, and he did it there in the place of his rejection and his pain. David was not afraid of Goliath – he was skillful with the sling and he knew what stones to work with. But, above all that, he knew he was coming at Goliath in the name of the Lord.

He knew he had learned to be skillful in the place his pain and rejection, and he knew he could do to Goliath what he had done with the lion and the bear.

David's promotion caused so much jealousy within the heart of King Saul that the king took the spear and the javelin and thrust it towards David. What you may not know is that Saul was a Benjamite. Benjamites were left-handed people and they could throw so accurately that they could actually split a hair with a spear. So, really, when he threw that javelin at David, David should not have lived. Yet, he did. Why? I believe it was all those times on the backside of the desert when he prayed to a living God. It was there, I believe, that he discovered the power of forgiveness. He said, in effect, "I'll forgive my dad because he didn't know what he was doing. I'll forgive my brothers because they didn't know what they were doing. I'll forgive anybody, Lord…"

Look back at the opportunity David had at the beginning of the chapter. You can imagine that David may have thought this was his God-given opportunity to deal with Saul. I believe God put Saul in a deep sleep to ask David, "What are you going to do? I put the enemy in your hand. Are you going to take vengeance? Are you going to take the very spear that was meant for your death and pierce him to the ground?" Even Abishai would encourage David to let him do it! We always have friends like that, don't we? We always have those who are all too willing to volunteer to execute vengeance when we hesitate to do it. Look at what David did, though. David had the audacity to say no. He knew Saul was already setting up his own downfall. David was determined not to touch God's anointed, saying he refused to touch the one where the oil once flowed. But, he did take the spear and the cruse of water. He took the weapon, the accusation, that was launched at him, the hate that was directed toward him, the thing meant to take him out, and he took it to the other side.

At the end of the story, we read that Saul recognizes David's voice, and David says, "God has given you into my hand, but I refused to lay my hand on the LORD'S anointed." He goes on to say, "May the LORD pay every man for his righteousness, his faithfulness, for the LORD delivered you into my hand today, but I would not stretch out my hand against the LORD'S anointed. Indeed, as your life was valued much this day and in my eyes, so let my life be valued" (see verse 24).

My prayer for you is that when you have an opportunity to strike and you have an opportunity to throw the javelin, that you don't. Friends, I have lived this out and it is not easy! This walk of love is tough! But, it comes down to the power of choice.

THE POWER OF A YOKE

Let me show you another element of this understanding. Oxen are referred to as burden-bearing animals. Yokes were used to help them to carry heavy loads. The owners would put the yoke on them when they were young, so that the oxen would grow into it and become accustomed to it. This is a picture of what often happens in our own lives – we do not realize that we have been carrying loads, possibly even from a young age, and we don't realize how ingrained it is until we are much older.

Unforgiveness is a learned behavior. Often, we find that we have learned a behavior that we think we have under control, only to discover that it has become a yoke. Unforgiveness gets control of you, then it becomes bitterness, then you become untrusting with everything, and eventually you become ugly, edgy, and hateful. You start stereotyping anything and everyone because of your situation.

I've been pastoring for many years and I've seen people's hurts turn into bitterness, then bitterness turns into hate, and then hateful people turn into ridiculous people. I know people serving time behind bars simply because they were tied into yokes they never dealt with. People start to play around with drugs, alcohol, pornography, etc., and the whole time they were telling themselves they had it under control. But, then "click!" The yoke attaches and suddenly, it has control of them. Once it has control, friendships, relationships, and marriages can be destroyed. Satan kept them ignorant of his devices. But, the good news is that the anointing through Jesus Christ is a yoke-destroying, burden-lifting anointing!

Look back at 1 Samuel 26:25 at what happened with David. Saul ended up saying to David, *"Blessed be thou, my son David: thou shalt both do great things and also shalt still prevail."* David was delivered out of every tight place, out of every troubled place, and out of every narrow place. David was delivered out of every situation that caused him harm. I really believe it was because he was a man of mercy and a man who had the ability to forgive. Absalom, his own son, was out to kill him. You can read the account in Psalm 3, where you find the words, *"How have they increased? How have they increased who troubled me?"* In essence, he's saying, "How have they increased who put me in a vice and put me in a tight and narrow place? For they say in their own heart and soul, there is no help for him in God." David rose up and said, *"But, thou, oh Lord, are a shield for me, the glory and the lifter of my head."* David cried out to God and God heard him and answered him out of His holy hill. Mercy will always, always triumph over judgment.

My desire is that your eyes and your life would be valued by the Lord and He would deliver you out of every tight place. I pray that this would happen because you didn't retaliate, because you did not hold grudges, and because you still had mercy when everything in you and everything around you said not to forgive someone, even when what they did was wrong. That shows your understanding, the place where the light has shone into darkness, of their value and yours – and I believe that causes God to deliver you from your tight places!

THE TWO PRIESTS

Let me tell you a story to illustrate this point. Two priests went to seminary together but ended up going to separate parishes. They went several years without seeing each other. One of the priests had an opportunity to go to the Vatican and meet the Pope. He was flown in for the weekend and was so excited about being at the Vatican that he prepared early for his scheduled dinner. You don't want to be late for dinner with the Pope, right? On his way to the Vatican, he came upon a deserted place where several homeless people were gathered. The friend paused, thinking one of the men looked like the man he went to seminary with, but he continued on his way. He passed by again and asked the man's name, telling him who he was, and it turned out to be his old friend!

He asked him what happened to him and the friend responded that he had experienced trouble in his parish and, instead of resolving it, he had gotten bitter over those situations and lost his ability to effectively serve there. It ultimately began to compromise his relationship with the Lord. He had decided to fly to the Vatican, thinking he could find some answers there, but he didn't find any. So, he started hanging out with the homeless population there. He was homeless himself and didn't let anyone know for years that he was even there. At the time his old friend bumped into him, he didn't even look like himself. He had a beard and hadn't showered in years. He had come to the Vatican seeking answers, but when he didn't hear what he wanted to hear, he became hopeless and, eventually, homeless.

The first friend invited him to join him at his dinner with the Pope, offering to let him come to his hotel to shower and get dressed. He hesitated, saying that he was not worthy to be around the Pope with the life he had been leading. When it was time for dinner, the friend explained to the Pope that he had found his old friend, sharing his story with him. The Pope agreed and as they ate together, he invited the homeless priest to speak with him privately. When the homeless priest stepped out, the Pope looked at him and said, "I must make confession to you." The priest initially refused, but the Pope replied, "Once a priest, always a priest." He made confession with him and the Pope restored the priest back to his original place. I believe he is still there now, serving the homeless community to which he used to belong. This was all because somebody showed mercy and forgiveness.

PLANTING OUR CHURCH

This story is a little more personal. When my wife and I planted our church in 2001, we were both so very excited. It wasn't long before it seemed like God was breathing on it and the church quickly grew to 300 people in four years, and we had to hire people to help. One of the ladies we hired was one of my own sisters, who served as our Children's Director. One mid-week, we had a powerful service, but there were some complications back in the kids' area. After everyone had picked up kids and we were all ready to go home, I spoke to my sister about what had happened that night. She proceeded to tell us about the incident, so I told her our policy for how we handle situations like this one – only to have her disagree with me. I told her that as the pastor of this church, it was my responsibility to establish policies and procedures for how we handle these kinds of problems. She and her husband at that time got offended and left the church.

This was gut-wrenching because it was our own family and we were very close. As time went on, it made family gatherings awkward and difficult, and we were trying to iron out our own feelings about what went on. God was really working on me and my wife about forgiving my sister and brother-in-law. So, we did, but things stayed the same until a few years had gone by and they announced that they were going through a divorce. My sister was devastated by this surprise, and she repented and got things right with me and my wife. She and her son even moved in with us for a year until they could get back on their feet. They say God works in mysterious ways, and I believe that to be true. Our relationship has been restored and we both learned that forgiveness is a powerful truth for God to recover what seems to have been lost.

My prayer is that God would reveal to you any areas of your life where you are holding people in unforgiveness, and that His light would shine in the dark places where ignorance wants to rule. I am reminded of the story in Genesis 32:25-26 where Jacob wrestled with the angel and prevailed. When the angel saw that he was not prevailing against Jacob, he touched the hollow of Jacobs's thigh. Jacob was seeking the blessing, but the blessing is not in holding on, it is in letting go!

We have the opportunity to stand as children of light, seeking knowledge and understanding. Darkness cannot comprehend the light, and Satan doesn't understand the Christ. Through God, we have the ability to rise above any situations or dilemmas in life that warrant vengeance, and instead choose mercy over judgment. The result is that the door to our own deliverance will be opened when we understand not to hold on to past hurts or offenses but to let them go to obtain the blessing.

May the revelation of this chapter help you move from a tight place to a forgiving place. As we embark into the next chapter, I pray that the Holy Spirit would lead you and direct you from your tight place to your safe place.

CHAPTER 3 - POWER POINTS

- We must be willing to show mercy to others, because God has already shown great mercy to us.
- The enemy occupies the darkness, the place of ignorance, but when the light shines into the darkness, we can overcome by the power of revelation.
- The power of a pardon is restorative!

CHAPTER 4

THE POWER OF A BLESSING
FROM A TIGHT PLACE TO A SAFE PLACE

I want to share with you now how we go from a tight place to a safe place. We've covered moving to the place of dominion, the place of grace, and the power of a pardon, and now I want us to look at the life of Jacob to understand this journey to a safe place.

THE DREAM

Jacob is first introduced to us in Genesis 25, where we read that, at his birth, he grabbed the ankle of his brother Esau. Later in his life, he convinced Esau to trade his birthright for a bowl of lentils and tricked his own father, Isaac, into giving him the blessing meant for the firstborn. In Genesis 27, we see Esau bitterly mad to the point where he is wanting to kill his own twin brother, Jacob, for stealing the birthright. When we catch up to Jacob later in Genesis 28, we find him running from Esau, after having tricked him out of both his birthright and his blessing, and Jacob continued running until he was at the point of exhaustion. He came to a certain place and, according to Genesis 28:11, *"He tarried there all night because the sun was set; and he took of the stones of that place, and put them for his pillows, and lay down in that place to sleep."* Verse 12 goes on to say, *"And he dreamed, and behold a ladder set up on earth, and the top of it reached to Heaven: and behold the angels of God ascending and descending on it."* This is where Jacob got the revelation of the safe place called Bethel, the house of God. It is there where God spoke to him and told him, in effect, "As I was with Abraham and your father Isaac, so I will be with you, through the good, the bad, the ugly."

THE BURDEN

Later in his life, Jacob worked in Laban's house and was mistreated and taken advantage of, having his wages changed ten times. But, God's blessing was still evident, even in the midst of Laban's corruption and heavy burden. Jacob came in empty-handed and left with the wealth of Laban, just as God had said. After departing from Laban's house, Jacob came back (in Genesis 35) and found the place God where had given him the dream and spoke about the blessing. Jacob reflected back on the twenty years of heavy labor and burden that had passed and saw the hand of God so mighty in it, he renamed Bethel to El Bethel, from "the house of God" to "the God of the house." He did this simply because he saw the hand of God deliver him from the burden to the blessing.

There is much to say about this story concerning the safe place that God has reserved for us, so let's break it down in more detail.

THE BIRTHRIGHT

The birthright was quite significant in those days, because if you were the firstborn, you had a right to a double portion of your father's inheritance, according to Deuteronomy 21:17. All sons have an inheritance, but the right of the firstborn son meant he received double. So, in the case of Jacob, his mother must have told him about the prophecy God gave to her concerning her sons while they were yet in the womb. You can find the prophecy in Genesis 25:23, where it says, *"And the Lord said unto her, 'Two nations are in thy womb, and two manner of people shall be separated from thy bowels; and the one people shall be stronger than the other people; and the elder shall serve the younger.'"* So, Rebekah had direct knowledge from God about what would eventually take place.

We find in Genesis 25:29-34 the story of how it all played out. Jacob was in the kitchen making beans and Esau was extremely hungry from being in the field hunting all day. Jacob offered him the bowl of beans in exchange for the birthright and verses 32-33 record, *"And Esau said, Behold, I am at the point to die: and what profit shall this birthright do to me?"* Jacob had him swear to it, and Esau sold his birthright unto Jacob. This matters because, as we will see, it is an important aspect of the blessing.

THE BLESSING

As we have just read, Jacob bought the birthright from his brother Esau by selling it for a pot of beans. Jacob could operate in the name of his brother Esau. We typically think that Jacob was a supplanter by stealing the blessing, but the reality is he had every right to it because Esau gave it up!

We see in Genesis 27 that when Isaac was about to die, he desired to eat some venison. He told Esau to go into the field and hunt for a deer so that he could eat it and bless him before he died. Rebekah seized her moment while Esau was away hunting. Isaac was blind and about to die. She remembered the word God had given her, that the elder would serve the younger. She told Jacob to quickly kill a goat and prepare it to taste just like venison, and to wrap its skin around his arms so that they would feel like Esau's arms. When the goat was prepared, they gave it to Isaac. Remember what I said earlier? Jacob had every right to come in his brother's name because of what he had obtained from him. So, Isaac said, "It sounds like Jacob, but feels like Esau..." Afterward, Isaac began to bless Jacob, telling Jacob what he will become, and that the God Who was with his father Abraham and with Isaac would be with him all the days of his life.

THE SAFE PLACE

After Isaac blessed Jacob, tremendous bitterness began to erupt from Esau (see verse 34), and he desired to slay Jacob. Isaac and Rebekah thought it would be best if Jacob went to Rebekah's brother Laban's house and perhaps marry one of his daughters. Jacob seemed to be running for his life in a terrain he did not know quite like his brother did. As he was running, he was thinking and imagining that at any given time Esau could come out of nowhere to surprise him and overtake him. He started to get tired, both physically and mentally. In Genesis 28:11, we see that, *"He lighted upon a certain place, and tarried there all night because the sun was set; and he took of the stones of that place, and put them for his pillows, and lay down in that place to sleep."*

It's amazing to me that the certain place Jacob lighted upon, according to most scholarship and Jewish teaching, is the exact same place Abraham came to over a hundred years earlier to build an altar to sacrifice Isaac. After a hundred years, the altar still remained intact. The stones were still marked with the DNA of the ram's blood that was caught in the thicket that God had provided. This was Abraham's safe place – the place of worship, the place of provision, the place where God preserved Jacob's father Isaac. God brought Jacob full circle to the same place where he would find safety, comfort, inspiration, and spiritual and practical direction. This altar that Abraham built is a type and shadow of what Jesus Christ did at the cross of Calvary, bringing safety, comfort, and provision. The blood of the Lamb, Jesus Christ, removed all sin, all sickness, all poverty, and death far from us who believe in His name.

THE DREAM IN THE SAFE PLACE

In Genesis 28:12-13, the Bible says, *"And he dreamed, and behold a ladder set up on the earth and the top of it reached to heaven: and behold the angels of God ascending and descending on it and, behold the Lord stood above it, and said I am the Lord God of Abraham thy father, and the God of Isaac: The land whereon thou liest, to thee will I give it, and to thy seed."* God brought Jacob from his tight place to his safe place to give him his placement as a son of God so that the dream he received could be articulated and demonstrated.

This safe place, the place of Christ's finished work, is a place where you and I receive and conceive what God has spoken. It's a place of strength and possibility. Jacob needed his own experience with God to solidify his birthright and his blessing. It was in that place, the safe place, where Jacob got the perseverance, motivation, and confidence to wake up and move toward his future. As Jacob awoke to a fresh possibility, he renamed the place that was called Luz to Bethel, "the house of God," calling it "the Gate of Heaven" and "the place where God dwells."

It's so crucial that we understand this safe place called "the house of God," the place where God abides and speaks. We live in a time when people everywhere, all across the world, are being de-sensitized to the Church, the house of God. Regardless of how you feel or believe, the Church is still Jesus' bride and vehicle to minister to a hurting world. Like Jacob discovered, it's the safe place where you can get instruction, direction, and inspiration for life's situations and problems. If you find yourself in a tight place, pray for God to order your steps and you will find that He will bring you full circle to a safe place called the house of God, the glorious Church of Jesus Christ.

THE SAFE PLACE IN THE DREAMER

We have talked a lot about the certain place, which I call the safe place, which was the place where God spoke to Jacob about his future. When Jacob took one of those stones and anointed it with oil and proceeded to make a covenant with God, he was not just anointing that safe place, but that safe place was going anywhere and everywhere he was going. That was the revelation! God was going with him, and God was going to bless him and his seed. Jacob received the revelation that he was in the safe place of God, the Church, the Bethel of God.

As Jacob journeyed upward toward Haran, in Genesis 29, where his mother's brother Laban lived, he came emptied-handed and all he had was a staff in his hand, a birthright, and his father's blessing – and a dream that God was with him. It was all he needed! As Jacob approached the city of his Uncle Laban, he came to a well to quench his thirst, and there he met the girl of his dreams. The story goes on to say that Jacob fell in love with Rachel and Laban told him he needed to work for him for seven years before he would give her to him. We know the story – Jacob worked for seven years and the time came when he should be getting married to Rachel, but he instead got Leah.

This is the beginning of a whole lot of family mess. You can already see Laban starting to take advantage of Jacob, but remember God is working for him. Jacob agreed to work another seven years for Rachael and the Bible says it seemed just like few days for Jacob (see verse 20). After the wedding with Rachel, Jacob started having babies with Leah, then the concubines, and then finally God opened up Rachael's womb.

It was evident that the hand of blessing was on Jacob, and Laban started to get jealous and changed Jacob's wages ten times! Jacob voiced his frustration to Laban, and Laban made a deal with him. What Laban didn't know was that God had given Jacob another dream concerning the flocks and the cattle. Jacob negotiated with Laban for all the speckled, spotted, and brown cattle.

From that moment on, you can see the providence of God working overtime on Jacob's behalf. All the cattle and flock begin to reproduce nothing but speckled, spotted, and brown babies, which all belonged to Jacob. The hand of God was upon Jacob, and he realized that the dream he had in the safe place was unfolding right before his very eyes.

Regardless of where you find yourself, in whatever tight places you feel trapped in, just know that you are not just in the house of God, but there is a God of the house who is working on your behalf so that you will experience the blessing of God.

THE PLACE CALLED MAHANAIM

We have covered Jacob's journey from the kitchen to the place of blessing, from the dream to the marriage, and from being ripped off to being exceedingly blessed. I want to talk to you now about a special safe place from any tight place called Mahanaim.

After God had given Jacob tremendous blessings from Laban's house, Jacob departed from the wilderness of Haran. God charged him to go back to his land, and Jacob kept thinking about Laban and Esau. He thought about Laban because he was leaving with all of Laban's wealth, and all of Laban's family, and, unbeknownst to him, one of Laban's gods. He left without Laban's blessing and Laban didn't know they were packing up and leaving and heading back toward Beersheba. When he did eventually find out, he got upset at Jacob and pursued him.

In Genesis 31:44-45, we find this exchange between Jacob and Laban: *"Now therefore come thou, let us make a covenant, I and thou; and let it be for a witness between me and thee. And Jacob took a stone, and set it up for a pillar."* In verse 49, it continues, *"He said, the Lord watch between me and thee, when we are absent one from another."* They made a covenant with each other and when they got done, according to Genesis 32:1-2, Jacob went on his way and the angels of God met him. When Jacob saw them, he said, "'This is God's host,' and called the place Mahanaim." This word means "double camp" or "two armies."[4]

---

4   Strong, James. "Mahanaim," Hebrew 4266. *Strong's Exhaustive Concordance of the Bible.* Iowa Falls, Iowa: World Bible Publishers, 1986.

This place called Mahanaim became a safe place for Jacob and his seed. Years later, we find David in his old age fleeing from Absalom, who was usurping authority and trying his best to seize the throne by force. It seems as though David could not do anything about it – he was old, and had been mandated by God to give the throne to Solomon. Absalom did not like that decision, so he tried to take it by force. Absalom had all the backing and was ready to kill his father, so David's mighty men took him and hid him in Mahanaim. You can find this story in 2 Samuel 17. What is so amazing to me is that when God is for you, it does not matter who is against you – you will always be protected and be at peace in a safe place!

When God gives you a dream, and in that dream He speaks destiny, instruction, direction, and inspiration, it's not just for you, but for your seed, as well. David was protected by the armies of God simply because of the promise He made with Abraham, Isaac, and Jacob hundreds of years prior. The Bible says in Galations 3:29, *"And if you belong to Christ, then are you Abraham's seed, and heirs according to the promise."* Beloved, I say to you today that if you find yourself in a tight place, call on the Lord of Hosts and you, too, like Jacob and David, will be preserved and protected in a safe place.

A PLACE CALLED JABBOK

Now I want to elaborate on the place called Jabbok. Going back to Jacob's story, we see that he has come a long way. But, the biggest giant he still had to face was confronting him. Jacob thought it was his twin brother, Esau, but as we will see, Jacob's biggest giant is Jacob! Jacob was afraid when he discovered that Esau was coming to meet with him, and this is where we pick up the story. Genesis 32:22 reads, *"And he rose up that night, and took his two wives, and his two women servants, and his eleven sons, and passed over the ford of Jabbok."* Now, this is very interesting to me because the word Jabbok means "the place of pouring forth," "empty out," and, by analogy, "to spread out (as a fruitful vine)."[5] When Jacob finally crossed the Jabbok, the Bible says he was left alone and there he wrestled with a man until the breaking of day (see verse 24). As Jacob wrestled, he prevailed, and when the man saw he could not

---

5   Strong, James. "Jabbok," Hebrew 2999. Strong's Exhaustive Concordance of the Bible. Iowa Falls, Iowa: World Bible Publishers, 1986.

prevail against Jacob, he touched Jacob in the hollow of his thigh, the place of reproduction. The man said, in verse 26, *"'Let me go, for the day breaketh,' and Jacob said, 'I will not let you go, except you bless me.'"*

Jacob had been on a journey for over 20 years, but there was still something in Jacob that was not settled and that was the blessing. The question that arises in me is, If Jacob had been blessed by his father and blessed by God at Bethel, why was he still seeking to be blessed when he already had the blessing? The answer to that question, I believe, is that we really never come to understand the blessing of God in our first birth or nature. In verse 28, the man told Jacob that his name was now Israel. His new name and nature could now emerge. Only Israel understands the fullness of the blessing.

Just like us, when we are born again, we receive our true nature found in Christ Jesus, and only in Christ will we really come to know the fullness of the blessing we have in Him. But, just like Jacob, we must come to the place called Jabbok where we become vulnerable and empty out all we think we are and are not and everything we think we can and cannot do. When you find your Jabbok, know that you have found a safe place where there will be a safe man waiting there for you, to wrestle until the breaking of a new day that will arise in your life, that will change your name, your nature, and eventually, your life.

A PLACE CALLED PENIEL

We next see Jacob moving on to the place called Peniel (see Genesis 32:30), which means "the face of God."[6] It's the place of transformation, where God changes your nature and your name. Jacob could not get delivered from himself until he wrestled with God and saw him face to face, and only then could there be transformation. God wrestled with Jacob until Jacob discovered the God in him, who would cause him to prevail and who would cause him to conquer every fear and insecurity in his life.

When Jacob finished his wrestling match, he was ready to confront his fear of his brother Esau. The greatest place to find yourself is in the safe place of the presence of God where he transforms you into His own image and likeness. Genesis 33:1 says, *"And Jacob lifted up his eyes, and looked, and, behold,*

---

6   Strong, James. "Peniel," Hebrew 6439. *Strong's Exhaustive Concordance of the Bible.* Iowa Falls, Iowa: World Bible Publishers, 1986.

Esau came, and with him four hundred men. And he divided the children unto Leah, and unto Rachel, and unto the two handmaids." Verse 4 says *"And Esau ran to meet him, and embraced him, and fell on his neck, and kissed him: and they wept.*" This is the result of two men allowing God to deal with their fears and shortcomings.

When you allow God to take you, like Jacob, from safe place after safe place to work in you and out of you what He needs, He will ultimately bring you to a place called Peniel, where you encounter God face-to-face and where He is able, in a moment, to bring transformation to your condition and move you from a tight place to your safe place.

Our next prophetic journey takes us from tight place to a blessed place where we learn more on the power of a blessing.

CHAPTER 4 – POWER POINTS

* The Church and presence of God are our safe places and He is always working on our behalf.
* God gives us dreams to help us in our journey.
* Transition and transformation come when you encounter God!

CHAPTER 5

THE POWER OF A BLESSING
FROM A TIGHT PLACE TO A BLESSED PLACE

In the previous chapter, I took you through the life of Jacob, who was running from his brother Esau and his father-in-law Laban. He came back to Bethel, the place where he had the revelation of the house of God. There, he had another revelation that God was with him and renamed that place El-Bethel, "the God of the house." He recognized that, regardless of whatever tight place he was in, God would always lead him back to a safe place. In this chapter, I want to show you about moving from a tight place to a blessed place.

BALAAM AND HIS DONKEY

In Numbers 22:20-35, we see the story of God speaking to a man named Balaam, telling him that, if men come to him, he is to go with them, but to do only what God tells him to do or say. Balaam went with the princess of Moab, but God's anger was aroused and the angel of the LORD stood in opposition to him. Balaam's donkey saw the angel standing in the road with a drawn sword and she turned aside, which made Balaam strike her. Then, the angel of the LORD stood in a narrow path, a tight place, and when the donkey saw the angel, she pushed herself against the wall, crushing Balaam's foot against it, causing him to strike her again. Then, the angel went further and stood in a tight place where there was no way to turn either to the right or to the left and the donkey saw the angel and laid down. Balaam struck the donkey a third time. Then, the LORD opened the mouth of the donkey, and she said to Balaam, "What have I done to you, that you have struck me these three times?"

Balaam answered, "Because you have made a fool of me. I wish I had a sword in my hand, for then I would kill you." The donkey continued, "Am I not your donkey, on which you have ridden ever since I became yours to this day? Was I ever disposed to do this to you?" And Balaam replied, "No." Then, the Lord opened Balaam's eyes and he saw the angel of the LORD standing in the way, with his drawn sword in his hand. He bowed down and fell on his face. The angel asked him, "Why have you struck your donkey these three times? Behold, I have come out to stand against you because your way is perverse before me. The donkey saw me and turned aside before me these three times. If she had not turned aside from me, surely just now I would have killed you by now and let her live." Balaam replied, "I have sinned, for I did not know that you stood in the way against me. Now, therefore, if it displeases you, I will turn back." But, the angel told him to go on, but to only speak the word of the LORD given to him.

I know that was a long introductory story, but it's important for understanding this idea of moving to a blessed place.

THE THREE SPIRITS

First, let's look at the book of Jude. In Jude 1:11 in the New Living Translation, it says, *"For they follow in the footsteps of Cain, who killed his brother. Like Balaam, they deceive people for money. And like Korah, they perish in their rebellion."* This Scripture helps us see that we as born-again Christians must overcome, by the grace of God working through our faith, these three spirits that seduce every believer: the spirit of Cain, which is the spirit that kills a brother; the spirit of Korah, which is the spirit of rebellion; and the spirit of Balaam, which is the spirit of deception or failure. Let's dig a little deeper and allow this revelation to unfold.

THE SPIRIT OF CAIN

Let me deal with the first two quickly, so we can focus more in-depth on the spirit of Balaam. The spirit of Cain is a brother-killing spirit. In Genesis 4, Cain brought a sacrifice of the produce of his land, while Abel brought a sacrifice from his firstlings of his flock. God favored Abel's offering, simply because he had a greater understanding of what God was requiring. Abel understood that

God was not asking for his best as much as He was asking for his first. Since God received Abel's offering and rejected Cain's offering, Cain, instead of making things right, allowed jealousy and envy to prick his heart, to the point that he eventually killed his brother.

Abel knew he could do nothing out of his own power and ability, but he knew to give God what He was requiring. So, as Abel gave God the firstling of his flock, he presented a lamb to the God he served, and God received it with gladness. Here we see a preview of Jesus, the Lamb of God, Who would be a firstling and Who would be the ultimate sacrifice of the ages, representing true worship unto God. Cain presented God his best, but not his first, and that caused God to reject his sacrifice. Because Cain was unwilling to repent, he allowed sin to creep into his heart.

This is a sad story in the Bible, but it shows us a problem that arises not just in families, but in churches, businesses, and schools all over the world. We learn a great lesson here about the God we serve – He wants the first and not the last, or even your best. Anytime you do anything out of the sweat of your own brow, as Cain tried to do, no matter how good it is or how good it looks, it still falls short of the glory of God if it is not your firstfruits.

The spirit of Cain is discord among brothers, and it is as old as Creation. It is amazing that within just a few years of the creation of Adam and Eve, we see the dynamic of Cain and Abel.

THE SPIRIT OF KORAH

Next is the spirit of Korah, which is the spirit of rebellion. In Numbers 16, we find Korah approaching Moses with 250 princes of the assembly, prominent men of the community. Korah proceeds to tell Moses that he has gone too far, and that it's not just Moses and Aaron who are set apart by the LORD but the whole community of Israel who is set apart. Korah goes on to ask Moses what right he has to act as though he is greater than the rest of the LORD's people. So, Moses replied to Korah and told him to take censers of fire and incense and that on the next day God would choose which one was holy. The next day came and Moses spoke that God would open up the earth and swallow the rebellion of Israel and bury them alive. Just as the words came off of his lips, the earth opened up and swallowed Korah and all his company.

Korah supposedly wanted to help Moses, but we see that it wasn't necessarily that he wanted to help, but more that he felt like he had an ability and gifting that he wanted to use to promote himself. We see this in the modern world as well as the modern church, too. People try to put titles and giftings on themselves that perhaps they don't fully possess or for which they aren't fully prepared. They lack the anointing to carry it out. The lesson that needs to be learned here is to stay in your lane rather than trying, like Korah, to promote yourself.

THE SPIRIT OF BALAAM

Now, let's get back to Balaam. The spirit of Balaam is the spirit of failure. His name means "failure of the people" and "brought to nothing."[7] Balaam was hired by the king of Moab to curse Israel because of the Moabites' fear of Israel.

We all have fears and phobias – whether it is the fear of failure, fear of the future, fear of dying, etc. This is why we try to turn our focus to God and not on ourselves. The more God-conscious we become, the more of the fear of God we have. The more self-conscious we are, the more the spirit of fear grips us. We must remember what the Word says, though, in 2 Timothy 1:7, *"For God has not given us a spirit of fear; but of power, and of love, and of sound mind."*

When I was 12 years old, I became intensely afraid of the dark, like many kids my age. No matter what I did, it seemed to get worse every year, to the point that I was 30 years old and still afraid of the dark! Now, how many of you know that if you're 30, married, and have two kids, that's a problem! I discovered through some great teaching that faith is faith when you open up your mouth and declare God's Word over a circumstance. So, I opened up my mouth and started declaring what God's Word said about me and that's when things began to turn. I finally had to confront my fear because I hated the way it made me feel and I decided to take my power back.

That's when I found out that you can't confront anything you are not willing to identify, and you cannot be delivered from anything you are unwilling to

---

7   Strong, James. "Balaam," Hebrew 1109. *Strong's Exhaustive Concordance of the Bible.* Iowa Falls, Iowa: World Bible Publishers, 1986.

confront. The moment you can identify your fear or problem, you can confront it and conquer it. You do that by declaring God's Word over yourself and your dilemma. You cannot be successful unless you are willing to identify the things you need to confront and conquer. Look again at David and Goliath. David never did identify Goliath as a giant! He identified him as an uncircumcised Philistine – he conquered him because he did not fight Goliath on Goliath's terms.

In that same year, it seemed like I was confronted with the spirit of death for the whole year. People I loved were dying, people I worked with were dying, and people I graduated from high school with were dying. It just seemed like I would be next, and I was fighting thoughts and imaginations wherever I went. I was sure I would be next! It wasn't until I got so sick and tired of this spirit harassing me, that I finally had the audacity to identify it and confront it, using God's Word and declaring over my life. When I did confront it, that thing broke off of me and now I can enjoy my life!

The lesson I learned from all this mess is that you can take your power back anytime you want. Take it back by identifying, confronting, and conquering whatever is harassing you. You conquer the same way Jesus conquered the devil by saying, "It is written" (see Matthew 4:4). I'm no longer afraid of dying because I know my assignment and everything I'm supposed to pour out in my lifetime!

WHEN YOU CATCH NOTHING

Luke 5 recounts an amazing story. Here, we see the multitudes pressing in around Jesus to hear Him speak. He saw two boats, but the fishermen had gone out to wash their nets. So, He got into Simon's boat, but it is significant in this account that it did not refer to it as Peter's boat. When you read the Scriptures, you have to understand the power of difference. Anytime Jesus is addressing His disciple as Peter or Simon, it's so we can see the two natures at work here. "Simon" means "hearing" and "like a reed easily shaken by the wind," similar to being easily startled.[8] The name "Peter" means "rock," referring to something solid, foundational, steadfast, and unmovable, something that is

---

8   Strong, James. "Simon," 4613. *Strong's Exhaustive Concordance of the Bible*. Iowa Falls, Iowa: World Bible Publishers, 1986.

here today and will still be here tomorrow.[9] Isn't it amazing that God would shift his name from something unstable to something stable?

Jesus got into Simon's boat and began to teach the multitudes from there. When He stopped speaking, He said to Simon in verse 4, *"Put out into the deep and let down your nets for a catch."* What I love about this is that is shows that Jesus is on the verge, balancing between two realms. Some theologians believe that Jesus was walking on the shoreline, which is notable because it's the place where earth, something stable, meets water, something unstable. I see it this way – He had one foot walking as the son of Mary, touching what is stable, but He is also the Son of God, able to walk on what is unstable. He has the ability as the son of Mary and as the Son of God to walk in both spheres at the same time. He's not afraid of what is practical and stable, and He's also not afraid of what is unstable. One side is possible and the other side is impossible, and Jesus is not afraid of either one! He can walk that fine line between the two.

It is amazing to me that Jesus got into Simon's boat. Simon was unstable. He had gone fishing, but hadn't caught anything. Remember what I told you Balaam's name means? It means failure and for something to come to nothing. Simon is experiencing a "Balaam moment," if I can say that. He had failed as a fisherman. But, the key is that Jesus is not afraid of our failure. He's not afraid of our nothingness. Jesus will take us back into the boat and take us back to the same place where we found nothing, where we toiled fruitlessly, where we were disappointed, discouraged, sick, tired, or distressed, because He wants us to conquer it!

One of the best antidotes for conquering fear, failure, distress, and trouble is resilience. Resilience is "the power or the ability to return to the original form or position after being bent, compressed, or stretched."[10] We are resilient because of Christ coming inside of us and making us alive in Him. We understand that it is no longer we who live, but Christ Who lives on the inside of us (see Galatians 2:20). This Christ, this God, this One is not going to leave us. He gave us the ability and the power, whenever we are stretched by circumstance, to go back to our original form and original position in Him. We can bend, bow, and be stretched, but still not break!

9   Strong, James. "Peter," 4074. *Strong's Exhaustive Concordance of the Bible.* Iowa Falls, Iowa: World Bible Publishers, 1986.

10 Dictionary.com. https://www.dictionary.com/browse/resilience. (Accessed March 2019).

The truth of the matter is that God is not scared. He's not scared of your disappointment, He's not scared of your discouragement, and He's not afraid of your nothingness. Jesus will bring you back out to the same place and show you something new. He is going to make sure that when you get back to that disappointed place, when you go ahead and launch your net again, you're going to catch something. And that "something" is going to satisfy you and those with you.

Paul reinforces this concept of resilience in 2 Corinthians 4:8, where it says, *"We're troubled on every side, yet not in distress. We are perplexed, but not in despair, persecuted but not forsaken, cast down, but we are not destroyed. Always carrying around in our bodies the marks of the Lord Jesus, the dying of the Lord so that the resurrection life of Jesus on behalf of us, in by and through us."* The next time you feel down and out, alienated, boxed in, lonely, etc., remember this resilience! If you feel like you're being stretched and bent, know that He Who abides on the inside of you is greater! Come back to your original state and your original position as a child of God.

This brings us back to Numbers 22 and Balaam. Let me elaborate a little further here. The word "donkey" there is "she-donkey." According to Strong's Old Testament Hebrew, it means "to continue in patience" or "continue in strength" and it's related to the concept of flow.[11] In fact, it is the same word used in the story of Saul searching for lost donkeys belonging to his father Kish, found in 1 Samuel 9. (In fact, "Kish" means "bow" or "bent" and is also related to "iniquity(sin)."[12]) When people get stuck in iniquity or sin and don't understand who they are, they lose their flow, they cannot continue in patience and strength, and they don't know they're resilient.

Now, look at Balaam. In him, we see that "failure" saddled "strength" and "patience." Remember that the donkey saw the angel of the LORD with a drawn sword, standing in the way three separate times, at one point crushing Balaam's foot against the wall of a narrow place.

This is what I believe this story is showing us: Failure has a walk, a journey, and a pathway. That's what the foot represents. So, what we see is that

---

11   Strong, James. "Donkey," Hebrew 860. *Strong's Exhaustive Concordance of the Bible.* Iowa Falls, Iowa: World Bible Publishers, 1986.

12   Strong, James. "Kish," Hebrew 7027. *Strong's Exhaustive Concordance of the Bible.* Iowa Falls, Iowa: World Bible Publishers, 1986.

the strength of God and the patience of God are wanting to crush the walk of failure!

But, why would the strength and the patience of God want to destroy the journey of failure? Because, if we don't do it, we see that the angel of the LORD is standing in the tight place! What I love about this is that it shows us that God is the God of our tight place. Our failure is out to curse, as Balaam's assignment was, and our failure is out to bring chaos, to bring us to nothing, and to make us idle. It wants us to be afraid of the past and the future, so that we stay stuck in the middle, doing absolutely nothing. Failure wants to keep us bound to yesterday's mistakes and keep us away from the future. It wants to keep us idle so that we do nothing in the now.

Understand, too, that the angel of the LORD is a theophany of Jesus Christ. Anytime we see the angel of the LORD in the Old Testament, it is a picture of Jesus Christ in the New Testament. Are you starting to see the picture? God loves you so much that He stands in the middle of your tight place and whenever your failure tries to saddle up, Jesus is in your midst! He is all-powerful and He stands in the middle of your troubled place, in the middle of your sick place, in the middle of your distressed place and, just like He did with Simon Peter, He'll transform that place into a blessed place.

If we keep reading, we see that Balaam was hired by Balak. Balak was the king of Moab. He was afraid because he had heard about the children of Israel, that God was promoting and elevating them. God gave them a promised land and they were possessing it. Their reputation was preceding them – they were prospering and multiplying, carrying the ark wherever they went, and they were not people you'd want to fight against. Balak's name means "waster" or "annihilator."[13]

I believe Balak is a picture of religion – religion that becomes the waster and destroyer of people's lives. As long as religion can keep you bound to the Law, it can keep you under the curse. That's what modern-day Balaks do. They stand behind pulpits and try to hire a Balaam, your failure, to keep you idle and to keep you feeling disqualified. But, I believe that's why Jesus stands in the

---

13 Strong, James. "Balak," Greek 904. *Strong's Exhaustive Concordance of the Bible*. Iowa Falls, Iowa: World Bible Publishers, 1986.

middle of your tight place. It's so no one else can fit in there! He makes sure there is no Balaam, no failure.

I am absolutely convinced that God will move you from a tight place to your blessed place. Jesus is standing with a sword drawn in His hand and He's not afraid of your enemy, He's not afraid of your sickness or disease, He's not afraid of your misfortune or disappointment, He's not afraid of your failed marriage, or that your kids are on drugs or pregnant – He's not afraid of any of it!

What stands out to me about Balak's story is how laughable it is. You simply can't curse what God has already blessed! That's why it's impossible for you to be cursed! The Bible says that a curse without a cause comes to no avail (see Proverbs 26:2). Once God has blessed you, you are blessed indeed! Though times might be tight, He's the covenant God Who stands in the middle of your tight place with a sword drawn, so that whenever anything tries to come and annihilate or destroy that blessing, He will destroy it for you. Isn't that amazing?

We see that Balak took Balaam three times, to three mountains, trying to get him to curse Israel. Balaam was able to look down the mountain and see the people dwelling in their tents. At that time, when the cloud by day and the fire by night began to move, everyone in the tribes had an assignment. When they set up camp at night, all of Israel would dwell in their tents. If you looked down at them from a high mountain, the formation of their tents was in the shape of a cross. Can you imagine what that must have looked like?

At the end of the story, Balaam could not curse what God had already blessed. I believe that God will move us from a tight place to a blessed place and this story shows us that when any of our failures come and look at the dwelling of who we are, they see a cross! They see the resurrected King and He is well able to deliver us from our tight places of trouble, sickness, and failure, and transform us into a redemptive blessed place. Hallelujah!

CHAPTER 5 – POWER POINTS

- The book of Jude shows us three spirits we need to overcome.
- Jesus operated in both the physical and spiritual realm – He's not intimidated by the impossible.
- God is not afraid of our failures! He wants to create a new walk of victory and blessing, redeeming the places where we have previously been afraid or have failed.

CHAPTER 6

THE POWER TO BLESS
FROM A TIGHT PLACE TO A POURING OUT PLACE

We learned in Chapter 5 about overcoming three spirits that hinder us from fully embracing the revelation of Jesus Christ. I am certain that when you can conquer the spirit of Cain, the spirit of Korah, and the spirit of Balaam, you will receive a fresh revelation of the in-dwelling Christ. As you receive that revelation, you will discover that the Blessed One abides on the inside of you, making you a very blessed person who cannot be cursed. The other side of this revelation is what I call "the switch," in that you will move from just being blessed to being able to pour out a blessing.

I believe that the next key to getting out of a tight place is found in a situation in the life of Jesus, recorded in Luke 24:50-51, after He talks about the promise of the Father, which is the Holy Spirit. It says, *"And he led them out as far as Bethany, and he lifted up his hands, and blessed them. And it came to pass, while he blessed them, he was parted from them, and carried up into heaven."* We also see in John 20:21 this passage: *"Then said Jesus to them again, 'Peace be unto you: as my Father hath sent me, even so send I you.'"*

The question that arises now is, What was Jesus sent by the Father to do? I believe that Scripture should interpret Scripture, so let's look at Acts 3:26. It says, *"Unto you first, God, having raised up His Son Jesus, sent Him to bless you, in turning away every one of you from his iniquities."* Wow! So, if I read it right, Jesus was sent by the Father to bless us, and Jesus says in John 20:21 *"As my Father has sent me, even so send I you."* To do what? To be a blessing!

God the Father sent Jesus, His Son, to be a blessing unto all humanity. And now, we are mandated by Jesus to do the same, following His pattern, and blessing as many people as we can with the in-dwelling Christ. Notice that Jesus did not get promoted or elevated to another dimension until He lifted up His hands and blessed them. So, here we see the pattern that Jesus left us. If you want to go to another level or dimension, then start pouring out blessing!

MAKING THE SWITCH

We can elevate ourselves from one dimension to another with the foundational principle Jesus laid out in the Scriptures above. We have to be the kind of people who learn to bless. At some point in our Christian walk, we have to make the switch of being blessed to being a blessing. One level is for me, the other level is for everybody else. I must come to the understanding that God has blessed me to be a blessing to others. Of course, it is easier said than done, but nevertheless, it needs to be understood.

First of all, you must know that God sent Jesus to bless you by removing sin, sickness, poverty, and death from you. That is the reason He died the death of the cross for all humanity, so that all humanity has the right to be saved if they believe in Jesus Christ. So, the first step in making the switch is understanding what Jesus Christ purchased at the cross for us. There is still power in His blood, power in His Word, and power in His name. Psalms 103:2 says, *"Bless the Lord, oh my soul, and forget not all his benefits."* The word "benefits" means "treatment" or "the thing he has given."[14] What an incredible thing God has given us! In fact, 2 Peter 1:3 says, *"According to his divine power hath given unto us all things that pertain unto life and godliness, through the knowledge of him that hath call us to glory and virtue."* That, my friends, is totally amazing!

With understanding comes the activation of your faith to receive all of God's promises. Faith is a vital part of you getting everything God has for you. I teach the people in my church about "beginning faith" and "finishing faith." Beginning faith is having faith to get saved, get baptized, get healed, and to prosper. Finishing faith is faith to get people saved, get people baptized, get

---

14 Strong, James. "Benefits," Hebrew 1576. *Strong's Exhaustive Concordance of the Bible.* Iowa Falls, Iowa: World Bible Publishers, 1986.

people healed, and to see people prosper. One is for you and the other is for everybody else! Until we can make the switch from being blessed to being able to pour out a blessing, our gospel remains narcissistic. It becomes about me, myself, and I, and that is only half the truth. We must have faith to finish strong. I believe that we are not in it to win as much as we are in it to finish! Let's finish strong by making the switch!

OVERCOMING THE HOUSE OF BETHANY

One of the things that hinders believers from operating in their blessing is condemnation. Now, I have been a pastor for over twenty years, and I can vouch that condemnation is the devil's babysitter. The word itself is a construction term related to something being uninhabitable, so when a house is condemned, you can't live in that house. That's the problem with most Christians – they fight the misery and affliction of condemnation. If you live a constantly condemned life, what you are saying, in essence, is that God can't live in you because you are uninhabitable. Think about what I just said. Jesus came in the likeness of sinful flesh, to condemn sin in the flesh, that the righteousness of the law might be fulfilled in us (see Romans 8:4). He died to come live in us, but He ever lives to come out of us! Jesus died so that He can forever make His abode on the inside of us, yet most Christians live such a condemned life, it's no wonder they struggle with being a blessing.

The Apostle Paul wrote in his epistle to the Romans in 8:1, *"There is therefore now no condemnation to them which are in Christ Jesus, who walk not after the flesh, but after the spirit."* We must overcome the lie of the enemy concerning condemnation in order to be the blessing Christ intended us to become. Jesus' blood removed all of your sins forever, so that we would never have to give in to the lie of condemnation.

Condemnation breeds misery and affliction. I say this because the word "Bethany" not only means "the house of dates or figs,"[15] but it also means, according to Hitchcock dictionary, "the house of affliction,"[16] and in the Ar-

---

15 Strong, James. "Bethany," Greek 963. *Strong's Exhaustive Concordance of the Bible.* Iowa Falls, Iowa: World Bible Publishers, 1986.

16 Hitchcock, Roswell D. "Bethany." *An Interpreting Dictionary of Scripture Proper Names.* New York, N.Y., 1869.

amaic, it means "the house of misery and poverty."[17] It's no wonder that in Luke 24:50, it says, *"And Jesus led them out as far as to Bethany, and Jesus lifted up his hands, and blessed them."* What I want you to see is that Jesus led them right to and through Bethany, the house of affliction, misery, and poverty, right through the misery of condemnation. Jesus knew exactly what He was doing! After all, He had just charged them to stay in Jerusalem until they had been clothed with power from on high, so that they could be blessed with all spiritual blessing and turn around to use that blessing to bless other who were in desperate need themselves. He was leading His people past their condemnation, and turning around and lifting up His hands and blessing them right in the middle of their affliction, misery, and poverty.

Let me tell you that if Jesus did it for them, He will do it for us, because He is not a respecter of persons (see Acts 10:34). If we are going to make the switch from being blessed to being a blessing, we will have to overcome the house of Bethany, which is our affliction, misery, and poverty caused by condemnation.

EMPOWERED TO BLESS

By grasping a greater understanding of the finished work of the cross, and by realizing what Jesus purchased through His death, burial, resurrection, and ascension, we will become powerful people who will demonstrate the love of God to all of humanity. Then and only then will we see His glory manifested in the earth through the treasure in earthen vessels, that the excellency of the power may be of God, and not us. Beloved, we live in a great time and God has predestined us to be conformed to the image of His Son (see Romans 8:29). According to Ecclesiastes 3:11, *"He has made everything beautiful in his time, and has set eternity in our hearts."* If we allow the truth of Christ in us, the hope of glory found in Colossians 1:27, we will become the house of blessing.

Until we fully understand that God has called us to become a blessing, we will remain idle. Notice that Jesus turned around and lifted up His hands and blessed the people, and when Jesus did that He was carried up to a whole different dimension.

---

17 Strong, James. "Bethany," Greek 963. *Strong's Exhaustive Concordance of the Bible.* Iowa Falls, Iowa: World Bible Publishers, 1986.

I believe there is a principle laid out in this, that if you are willing to bless and not curse in the dimension you are in, you will find promotion. You can see this also in the life of the patriarch Joseph, who, after he was sold to the Ishmaelites by his brothers, and sold again to Potiphar by the Ishmaelites, and then wrongly accused by Potiphar's wife, found himself in the lowest low, the prison (see Genesis 37-39). Joseph could have stayed bitter, angry, and resentful, but he held onto the dream. He could have thrown in the towel and said, "Forget this!" But no, he kept his faith toward his God, believing somehow, and somewhere, God would come through. Joseph stayed faithful to his God, and to his God-given gift. He was faithful to interpret dreams in the prison. He didn't have to do that, but he did! Because he was faithful in blessing the butler in a low, disgusting place, God blessed him by promoting him to the palace. In one moment, he is in a low place, and the next moment Joseph found himself in a high place, because he remained faithful with his gift.

God has blessed you with gifts, too. Use them to be a blessing, just like Joseph, and you will discover that God will make room for your gift, and bring you before great men (see Proverbs 18:16). Remember, promotion is found in blessing, not cursing, so the next time you find yourself in a low place, don't quit or become bitter or even angry. Stay committed to your God, to your dream, and to the God-given gift He gave you, and you will always be empowered to bless.

NO MORE EXCUSES

We have learned to make the switch from being blessed to being a blessing and to overcome the house of Bethany by grasping a greater understanding of the finished work of Jesus Christ on the cross. We learned that we have been empowered by the indwelling Christ, and we are responsible to bless at whatever level we find ourselves in, so that we can be promoted by God.

Knowing all of this great truth is wonderful, so now I'm removing the excuses! As I tell people all over this great world, you will love and hate the day you ever met me, because I spend a whole lot of time removing people's excuses. I have come to realize that where there is an excuse, there you will find a lack of desire. It's not that the excuse has bad intentions, it's that the excuse is keeping you from your promotion.

Desire is more powerful than talent, more prolific than gifting, and more dangerous than ability. I have always said, give me somebody who is full of desire, and I will pick him over somebody who is more qualified in talent, gifting, and ability. Desire to me is more powerful than all of that – desire has no quit in it, desire is never full, and it always stays hungry and thirsty for more. Desire is like what Solomon said in Proverbs 30:15-16, *"The horseleech has two daughters, crying, Give, give. And there are three things that are never satisfied, yes, four things that say it is not enough: The grave, and the barren womb; the earth that is not filled with water; and the fire that says it's never enough."*

Let's first start with the horseleech, or as they say in the south, bloodsuckers. Once on you, these are very difficult to get off. They have one purpose and that is to suck the life right out of the thing they're attached to. I liken the leech to desire, because once you have desire, it will stick and suck the life right out of that thing. Notice that the horseleech cried out "give, give" just like desire crying out, "Give me what's mine, give me what's mine. God, I won't stop until you give, give." Next, I liken desire to the grave that says it's never enough. The grave has never complained that it was full. It always has its mouth open to devour its next victim. And, just like the grave, desire is never full – it's always wanting more and more and more. The barren womb is the same. Like every little girl who desires a baby someday, so is desire expectant, always hoping and believing and never wavering. It's just like the earth that is filled with water, but it never says, "I have had enough." Or, like the fire that is devours the forest and anything that gets in its way, so is desire! Desire stays hungry and thirsty always, at all times. As long as you stay persistent like a leech, deadlier than a grave, more expectant than a barren womb, thirstier than an ocean, and hungrier than a fire, you will remove every excuse that comes your way that would sway you from the purpose of almighty God! Desire is the power that eliminates every excuse known to man. Let's come to the place where we have no more excuses!

AS HE IS, SO ARE WE IN THIS WORLD

In 1 John 4:17, it reads, *"Herein is our love made perfect, that we may have boldness in the day of judgment: because as he is, so are we in this world."*

Notice it says, "as he is," not as he was, or as he will be, but as Jesus *is*, so are we. This is a wonderful truth to come to understand, because when you grasp the revelation of "as Jesus is," the question becomes, "How is Jesus now?" Jesus is not sick, Jesus is not poor, Jesus is not stressed, Jesus is not mad, Jesus is not diseased, Jesus is in His right mind, Jesus is sitting on His throne, Jesus is full of love, Jesus is full of peace, Jesus is full of grace, etc. You get the point! Jesus is full of all authority, all power, and all dominion.

Many people think that God's intention was for us to go to heaven. Listen, I love heaven. I think it sounds like a wonderful place. But, I also think that if God only intended for us to go to heaven, He would have just left us there. He loved us and wanted to invest in us to make the earth like heaven. We bring heaven to earth when we act like our Father and use His power to pour out blessings, when we speak the words of life and truth over our situations, and when we allow Him, by His immeasurable power, to move through us!

Let us become so aware of the God we serve and allow that awareness of Him to determine what we receive from Him. We have to learn to speak grace and truth to people. Remember that, according to 1 Peter 4:8, love covers a multitude of sin. That's a multitude of "stuff" – weaknesses, shortcomings, failures, and faults. If we quit pointing the finger at people and start loving people, it will allow God's love to compel them. The goodness of God leads men to repentance, not us condemning them (see Romans 2:4). Our responsibility in this life is to bless. Jesus is One Who blesses, and so are we. Jesus is a peacemaker, and so are we.

The Father did not hold back His best, His only begotten Son. Romans 8:32 says, *"He who did not spare his own Son, but gave him up for us all – how will he not also, along with him, graciously give us all things?"* Do you see that? If the Father did not fail to give you the *best* that He had, what makes you think He will withhold the *rest* that He has? If He gave you the best thing, then you are entitled to the rest! This is how we move from the tight place to the power to bless place – the Father wants to make sure His sons and daughters get not just the best, but also the rest.

As we have learned in this chapter, there is a power to bless and to move from a tight place to a pouring out place. Next, we move forward in our prophetic journey, moving from a tight place to a yes place.

CHAPTER 6 – POWER POINTS

- One level of blessing is for us, the next level is for others. We need to move from being blessed to being a blessing!
- Promotion is found in blessing, not cursing.
- God gave us His best to give us access to the rest.

CHAPTER 7

THE POWER OF A SLING AND A STONE
FROM A TIGHT PLACE TO A YES PLACE

We have journeyed through many tight places in the last six chapters, discovering that God has answers for every tight and troubled place in which we find ourselves. God has provided tremendous solutions for all of us who believe in His Son. I want to shine light now on the power of a sling and a stone, moving us from a tight place to a "yes" place. In this chapter, I hope to empower you through the familiar story of David and Goliath, to show you that God is able to do exceedingly, abundantly, above anything you are able to ask, think, or even imagine, according to the power that works in you (see Ephesians 3:20). I also want you to see through the revelation of Jesus and His finished work of the cross that there is nothing that can stop the seed in you from accomplishing the purpose and the call on your life.

"So it was, when the Philistine arose and drew near to meet David, that David hurried and ran toward the army to meet the Philistine. Then David put his hand in his bag and took out a stone; and he slung it and struck the Philistine in his forehead, so that the stone sank into his forehead, and he fell on his face to the earth. So, David prevailed over the Philistine with a sling and a stone, and struck the Philistine and killed him. Therefore, David ran and stood over the Philistine, took his sword and drew it out of its sheath and killed him, and cut off his head with it. And when the Philistines saw that their champion was dead, they fled."

1 Samuel 17:48-51

CAN'T VERSUS CAN

Remember the passage we covered in Genesis 4:1-8 about Cain killing his brother Abel? I'm going to take a bit of liberty here with Cain. He is the first-born son to Adam and Eve and for our purposes here, I am going to call him "Can't" or "Inability" because Cain could not repent when God asked him to. Abel is the second son of Adam and I am going to call him "Ability" or "Can" because he was able to bring God a sacrifice that was well-pleasing to Him. In this story, Cain ("Can't" or "Inability") kills Abel ("Can" or "Ability"), and this is a pattern we see in the Bible and in life – your inability will always try to kill your ability.

In Genesis 6:4, we read, *"There were giants on the earth in those days, and also afterwards, when the sons of God came in to the daughters of men and they bore children to them. Those were the mighty men who were of old, men of renown."* Here we see where the sons of God impregnate the daughters of men. To fully understand this revelation, you must see the parallel I am making with the sons of God and the daughters of men. The sons of God denote the ability of God, just like Abel (Can), and the daughters of men represent Cain or Can't. With this in mind, you can see that when your Can impregnates your Can't, you produce giants in your land (your mind). Giants will always keep you from possessing your promised place, by fear, intimidation, and continual accusation. By understanding this, we can see a clear picture of how your Can't always wants to annihilate your Can.

In Numbers 13, Moses had twelve spies go up and investigate the promised land. Ten of the spies came back with an evil report, saying that the giants were too big and too strong and that they were not able to possess the land. Caleb and Joshua, men of a different spirit said, in verse 30, *"Let us go up at once and possess this land, for we are well able to overcome it!"* Again, we see where the children of Israel give in to the fear of the giants, and forfeit their Can with their Can't. After all, it was God Who said, in effect, "I have given you a land that flows with milk and honey. All you have to do is possess it." If God says it, that means He has given you the ability to possess it! But, the problem with the children of Israel was with their thinking.

THE PRINCIPLE OF PERSPECTIVE

I have discovered over the years, as it relates to the principle of perspective, that how you think will determine where you stand/understand; where you stand/understand will determine where you sit; where you sit determines what you see or do not see; and, what you see will determine what you will have or not have. The children of Israel couldn't have what God wanted them to have simply because they couldn't see what God had prepared for them.

In Matthew 23:2, Jesus says, *"The scribes and the Pharisees sit in Moses' seat."* Ephesians 2:6 says, *"And has raised us up together, and made us sit together in heavenly places in Christ Jesus."* Here we see that there are two seats available: Moses' seat and the seat of grace. Moses' seat speaks of the Law, which disqualifies you and tells you all the reasons you can't do something or possess your promise. The other seat is the seat of grace, which belongs to Christ, and it represents ability or favor. The seat God has called us to is the seat of grace, which gives us the ability to possess our promised place and move from any of our tight places.

In 2 Corinthians 3:6, we see this passage: *"Who also hath made us able ministers of the new testament; not of the letter, but of the spirit: for the letter kills, but the spirit giveth life."* God has made us able ministers of the New Testament, not of the letter, which is the Law, but the Spirit, which is grace. Hallelujah!

AS A MAN THINKS, SO IS HE

Going back to Numbers 13, the children of Israel couldn't possess their promised place because they were still sitting in their tight place, which was causing them to see themselves differently than how God was seeing them. The children of Israel saw themselves as grasshoppers. When your thinking is off, your position and perspective will be off. Proverbs 23:7 says, *"As a man thinks in his heart, so is he."*

God, by sending His Son to die on an old rugged cross, gave you and me the ability to possess our promised places. Don't give in to the lie of religion or the lie of a circumstance that holds you to your past. God sent Jesus to redeem us and restore us to our prominent place of His grace, to empower and enable us to do and possess what we couldn't do or possess for ourselves.

In 1 Samuel 17:33, when Saul is trying to disqualify David, the Bible says, *"And Saul said to David, 'You are not able to go against this Philistine to fight with him; for you are a youth, and he is a man of war from his youth.'"* What is so interesting to me about this is that the name Saul means "asked" and the root word means "to beg."[18] The reason this is so significant is that in Galations 4:9, it says, *"But now after you have known God, or rather are known by God, how is it that* you turn again to the weak and beggarly elements, to which you desire again to be in bondage?" Paul is writing to the people and saying, in effect, "Listen up guys, you have gotten to know God by His grace, why are you turning back to the beggarly elements of the Law, which only disqualifies you and tells you what you can't do and have?"

In essence, in 1 Samuel 17:33, Saul is a type of the Law, disqualifying David from his promotion. I love what David says back to Saul, in verse 34-37, when he responds that he used to keep his father's sheep and protect them from lions and bears. Goliath, he said, was an uncircumcised Philistine who would be just like the lions and bears, and he was confident that God would deliver him into his hands in the same way. Saul replied, "Go, and the Lord be with you!"

David, whose name means "love,"[19] responded back to the Law (Saul), saying, in effect, "You can't disqualify me, I know who my God is. And the same God Who delivered me from the paw of the lion and the same God who delivered me from the paw of the bear, will deliver me from the hand of this uncircumcised Philistine." In our own journey, there will be all kinds of people and all kinds of situations that will come and scream at us, telling us of what we can't do, can't have, and can't be. If that is the case in your journey, allow love to arise in your heart to silence the fears, intimidation, and accusations of your past. Remember, love never, ever fails!

---

18 Strong, James. "Saul," Greek 4549. *Strong's Exhaustive Concordance of the Bible.* Iowa Falls, Iowa: World Bible Publishers, 1986.
19 Strong, James. "David," Hebrew 1732. *Strong's Exhaustive Concordance of the Bible.* Iowa Falls, Iowa: World Bible Publishers, 1986.

THE ROCK THAT FOLLOWED THEM WAS CHRIST

Our Savior has qualified you, so take back your power to become and possess what He says you can become and possess! There are always highs and lows, but what stands true is God's Word concerning you.

In Numbers 20:7-8, God told Moses to speak to the rock and the rock would gush water to quench the thirst of the people and their animals. In 1 Corinthians 10:4, we find Paul saying to the people that the rock that Moses struck twice, and waters of refreshing that came out of it, was Christ. Another reference to a rock is found in Revelation 2:17, where we find this passage: *"He who has an ear, let him hear what the Spirit says to the churches. To him who overcomes I will give some of the hidden manna to eat. And I will give him a white stone, and on the stone a new name written which no one knows except him who receives it."* The first exhortation we get is that if we have any ability to hear, to hear what the third person of the Godhead is saying. So, the Holy Spirit says that if you overcome, which is grasping the understanding of death, burial, resurrection, and ascension, He will give to you hidden manna (revelation) of a white stone, and on that stone a new name will be written which no one knows except him who receives it.

The word "stone" here in the Strong's concordance means "smooth stone of verdict."[20] In Bible days, the courts would be set up outside the camp. If you were convicted of your crime by the mouth of two or three witnesses, you would be condemned and given a smooth black stone. If you were acquitted by the judge and the jury, you would be given a smooth white stone. This is very important to understand for the story as we move forward.

The book of Exodus details the usage of the Urim and Thummim, which were the stones found in a pouch of the ephod, under the breastplate of the high priest (see 28:29-30). Some scholars believe that one of the stones was white and the other was black, speaking of the yes and the no of God. This is why David asked for the ephod in 1 Samuel 30:7-8 when he was seeking the LORD's strategy. After the enemy had captured their wives and children, David was in a tight place and he asked where the ephod was because he needed to know what to do, considering his own men wanted to kill him. So,

20 Strong, James. "Stone," Hebrew 5586. *Strong's Exhaustive Concordance of the Bible.* Iowa Falls, Iowa: World Bible Publishers, 1986.

David inquired of the LORD, whether or not he should pursue and overtake and God said, "Yes, pursue and overtake, for you will without fail recover it all!" He went from a tight place to a yes place in a moment.

THE BROOK OF INHERITANCE

Knowing that the white and black smooth stones represented the yes and no of God, let's look at 1 Samuel 17:40, which says, *"Then he took his staff in his hand; and he chose for himself five smooth stones from the brook, and put them in a shepherd's bag, in a pouch which he had, and his sling was in his hand. And he drew near to the Philistine."* This is where the story gets really good! David understood that with God on his side, he could win. David ran toward the giant of fear, intimidation, and accusation, stopping by the brook to pick up five smooth stones. The word "brook" means "inheritance."[21] The brook represents God's inheritance that He has given unto us. Remember that 2 Corinthians 1:20 says, *"For all the promises of God in Him are Yes, and in Him Amen, to the glory of God through us."*

So, David picked up five smooth "yeses" from the brook of inheritance where all of God's promises are yes and amen. He put them in a shepherd's bag and moved toward the uncircumcised giant. So, what was the significance of the bag? We know that the number five represents God's grace, favor, and ability. David knew exactly what was going to happen when he put those five yeses in his shepherd's bag. The word "bag" in Strong's is the word "kaliy," which means "something prepared," but the Hebrew word comes from the root word "kalah," which means "something finished!"[22] Are you seeing it yet? David put the five smooth stones, of God's grace, in a "finished work."

It is no wonder that it only took one smooth stone to kill Goliath, because when David reached into the place of the finished work, there would only be one stone which would represent all other stones. That is the Christ, the Chief Cornerstone, that would crush the head of the uncircumcised giant who forever tries to intimidate with fear, intimidation, and false accusation!

---

21 Strong, James. "Brook," Hebrew 5158, root 5157. *Strong's Exhaustive Concordance of the Bible*. Iowa Falls, Iowa: World Bible Publishers, 1986.
22 Strong, James. "Bag," Hebrew 3615. *Strong's Exhaustive Concordance of the Bible*. Iowa Falls, Iowa: World Bible Publishers, 1986.

The patriarch David, the psalmist of Israel, paved way through his tight place to his yes place, and we, too, take what He has finished and pull out the Christ, the Rock of Ages. Wow!

THE POWER OF THE SLING

The word "sling" is the word "qela," which means "a hanging."[23] Remember from earlier in the book that every door that opens and closes has been hung correctly. Jesus, according to John 10:7, is the door, and according to Psalm 118:19 and Revelation 3:8, Jesus is the open door of righteousness. He is that door because he was hung "right."

So, if we read 1 Samuel 17:50, knowing what we know about the sling and the stone, we would read it like this: David prevailed over the Philistine with the hanging of the Christ that was in David's hand. My friends, you will continue to have victory after victory in your tight places when you understand what's in your hand. The word "hand" in the Hebrew means "power."[24] The power that Christ has given all believers all over the world is His finished work at the cross. Let's use it for destroying insecurities and inabilities, our "can't," in our own minds, so that we can possess our promised places, our "can," and make a difference in the world!

The power has been provided through the finished work of the cross. My prayer is that you've been inspired through this journey through the story of David and Goliath to possess your promised places by understanding the finished work that Jesus provided.

In the next chapter, we will cover the power of prophecy that will move you from a tight place to a resurrected place.

CHAPTER 7 – POWER POINTS

- Your "can" will always be at odd with your "can't."
- When your thinking is off, your position and perspective are also off.
- The finished work of the cross gives us the power to prevail.

---

23 Strong, James. "Sling," Hebrew 7050. *Strong's Exhaustive Concordance of the Bible*. Iowa Falls, Iowa: World Bible Publishers, 1986.
24 Strong, James. "Hand," Hebrew 3027. *Strong's Exhaustive Concordance of the Bible*. Iowa Falls, Iowa: World Bible Publishers, 1986.

CHAPTER 8

THE POWER OF PROPHECY
FROM A TIGHT PLACE TO A RESURRECTED PLACE

My goal in this chapter is to reveal the power of your voice. Understanding the power of your voice through prophecy will help you navigate through difficult times and empower you to release what God has put in your heart. Embracing the power of prophecy will cause you to speak to dead or seemingly impossible situations or conditions and see resurrection come to those areas.

In this chapter, we will see God unfold Israel's purpose and destiny through the power of prophecy, bringing resurrection to dead and dry bones. My heart is for you to see that Jesus is the same today, yesterday, and forever (see Hebrews 13:8), and that, if you're facing any dead or dormant thing, you can speak life to it.

Let's use the story found in Ezekiel 37 to help us reveal these truths, so that we can move from a tight place to a resurrected place through the power of prophecy. Are you ready?

THE HISTORICAL BACKGROUND

The vision that Ezekiel had dates back to the period of Israel's history known as the Babylonian Exile. In 597 BCE, the armies of Babylon forced Jerusalem to be under their control (see 2 Kings 24:10-16). Ten years later, Jerusalem rebelled again, so the Babylonians tore down Jerusalem and its temple and deported a second wave of Judean leaders. Ezekiel, whom God had called to the office of the prophet, was among the first wave of captives. For a decade,

Ezekiel and God's people had been under the regime of the Babylonians, who stripped away their identity, their faith, their temple, and their God. The people of God began to question if the God they had served and worshipped had been defeated by the Babylonian gods. So, God had a few prophets like Ezekiel who would remind the people that God was still God and that He was faithful even in the midst of captivity.

THE VISION

In Ezekiel 37, we see where God gives the prophet a vision. The vision is in direct correlation to the cry of desperation of God's people. In verse 1, we see that God's hand comes upon Ezekiel, whose name means "God will strengthen," "God will heal," and "God will recover," according to Strong's."[25] Can you see the picture here? God's strength, His healing power, and His ability to cause things to recover, are about ready to be tightly placed in a dead, dry valley with a whole lot of dead, dry bones. In verse 2, God places Ezekiel right in the middle of the open valley, where he sees the dry bones. God then asks the question that Ezekiel is dreading: "Can these bones live?" Ezekiel responds, "Oh, Lord God, only you would know, and only you are capable of restoring these bones." God commands Ezekiel to prophesy to the bones to hear the word of the Lord. What follows is a great rattling and coming together. In verse 9, God commands him to prophesy to the wind, and it brings life back into the bones, which become a great, exceeding army! God commands Ezekiel to prophesy yet one more time, this time to bring resurrection power to get up and go back to the land God has always had for them.

This vision Ezekiel had helped him understand that God is the God of all of our tight places, and that regardless of what seems to be going on at the time, He is for us and, according to Romans 8:31, if He is for us, who can stand against us? God was reassuring Ezekiel that all He needed was someone to stand in the gap and prophesy life and let Him do the rest. God will do the same for us, if we just learn the power of prophecy!

---

25 Strong, James. "Ezekiel," Hebrew 3168. *Strong's Exhaustive Concordance of the Bible.* Iowa Falls, Iowa: World Bible Publishers, 1986.

DRY BONES

When God put Ezekiel in the middle of the valley full of bones, Ezekiel looked around and he observed one thing, and that was that the bones were very dry. This is important is because the word "dry" is the word "yabesh" in the Hebrew, which means "to be ashamed, confused, or disappointed."[26] These bones that Ezekiel saw weren't just dry, they were very dry! That means these bones were very ashamed, very confused, and very disappointed.

The Bible says in Proverbs 29:18, *"Where there is no vision, the people perish."* The word "perish" means "naked" or "to uncover."[27] Nakedness always points to shame, and shame points to fear. When Adam and Eve were in the Garden, they partook of the Tree of the Knowledge of Good and Evil, which shows us a type of the Law that keeps us blinded to a relationship with God. When they ate of the forbidden fruit, their eyes opened and they knew they were naked, so they sewed fig leaves together and made themselves aprons to cover up their nakedness. They then heard the voice of God walking in the garden in the cool of the day, but they were afraid to communicate with the God who created them because they were naked. God confronted Adam and asked, "Who told you that you were naked?" And God said unto Adam, "Have you eaten from that tree that I told you not to eat?" (see Genesis 3).

Nakedness is shame, disappointment, and confusion. It breeds fear. Can you see it now? In Ezekiel's time, the children of Israel had no vision and no covering. It was no wonder they were losing faith and hope in their God!

Let's take a further look at what is the meaning of "bones." The word figuratively means "substance."[28] In Hebrews 11:1, we see that, *"Faith is the substance of things hoped for and the evidence of things not seen."* So, the bones that are very dry speak of Israel's faith that was very ashamed, disappointed, and confused. We see that God used Ezekiel to recover all was uncovered, and to prophesy to the faith of Israel to come together and unify. And that's exactly what happened! Ezekiel began to prophesy to the dry bones

---

26 Strong, James. "Dry," Hebrew 3002. *Strong's Exhaustive Concordance of the Bible*. Iowa Falls, Iowa: World Bible Publishers, 1986.

27 Strong, James. "Perish," Hebrew 6544. *Strong's Exhaustive Concordance of the Bible*. Iowa Falls, Iowa: World Bible Publishers, 1986.

28 Strong, James. "Bones," Hebrew 6106. *Strong's Exhaustive Concordance of the Bible*. Iowa Falls, Iowa: World Bible Publishers, 1986.

and as he did, the bones began to come together one by one to make up this exceeding great army.

Ezekiel 37:8 records that sinews and flesh came up upon them, and the skin covered them, but there was no breath in them. The word for "sinews" means "to overcome by gathering,"[29] and the word for "flesh" is "good news."[30] This passage paints a clear picture of God's redemptive power through prophecy, where the prophet ("God will recover") prophesies to the bones ("faith"), which are uncovered and full of shame, confusion, and disappointment, which causes a rattling and a coming together. God wraps the faith with the gospel of good news that will help overcome disappointment and fear. Selah!

THE POWER OF PROPHECY

When God made Man in His image and likeness, He gave Man the power to shift and change things, atmospheres, and situations simply through a spoken word. Oftentimes, though, circumstances keep us from demonstrating and activating this precious gift God has given to the believer. Prophecy is simply expressing the heart of God. It is also the spirit of affirmation. The word "affirm" means "to be made strong."[31] and the opposite is "infirm," which is "to be made weak."[32] God wants us to be vessels of affirmation, making strong those who are weak.

Prophecy is also one of nine gifts of the Holy Spirit, and it allows one to speak like God. I said earlier that we are created in His image, which means that we look like God, but we are also created in His likeness, which means that we can do what He can do. Since our God used His voice for creation, we have the ability to create in our world what we desire to see in it. Proverbs 18:21 says, *"Death and life are in the power of the tongue, and those who love it will eat its fruit."* Jesus also said in Matthew 15:11, *"It is not what goes into the mouth that defiles a person, but what comes out of the mouth; this defiles a person."* We have a responsibility to be creatures of light and not darkness, and we must use our voice to create life and not death. We also have

---

29 Strong, James. "Sinews," Hebrew 1464. *Strong's Exhaustive Concordance of the Bible.* Iowa Falls, Iowa: World Bible Publishers, 1986.

30 Strong, James. "Flesh," Hebrew 1319. *Strong's Exhaustive Concordance of the Bible.* Iowa Falls, Iowa: World Bible Publishers, 1986.

31 Dictionary.com. https://www.dictionary.com/browse/affirm. (Accessed March 2019).

32 Dictionary.com. https://www.dictionary.com/browse/infirm. (Accessed March 2019).

a responsibility to speak as the oracles of God (see 1 Peter 4:11) and call those things that are not as though they were, according to Romans 4:17.

One more principle about the power of prophecy is found in Mark 11:23, where it says, *"For assuredly, I say to you, whoever says to this mountain, 'Be removed and be cast into the sea,' and does not doubt in his heart, but believes that those things he says will be done, he will have whatever he says."* What I want you to grasp from this particular text is that it's important for you to speak to your mountain, because your mountain knows your voice. Your mountain will respond better to you because it's your mountain, and my mountain will respond better to my voice. So, don't be afraid of your mountain! Open up your mouth and let it hear your voice!

The story in Ezekiel 37 is so profound to me because Ezekiel was right in the middle of the captivity, and God asked him a question. Can these bones live? You can feel Ezekiel squirming – when God asks a question, it's not that He wants to know, but He is wanting you to know what He has always known! Here, Ezekiel is ten years into this captivity, with no hope of getting free, no faith to believe, and no vision of the future, and God steps down out of eternity, and into time, and says, in essence, "There is nothing too hard for me. In fact, I will use your voice to help me bring a hope and a future back to these confused and disappointed bones. So, Ezekiel, I need you to prophesy to these shameful, confused, and disappointed bones and prophecy to their faith and say, 'I will cause breath to enter you, and you will live!'"

Now, we come to the end of the story, where the bones have aligned and look like an army. Ezekiel was commanded to prophesy again, this time to the wind of the four corners of the earth, to breathe upon the slain. There is so much in this text – after God had formed man, man's bones were attached, and man's sinews, flesh, and skin were attached, but there was no life until God breathed in man. God prophesied life, destiny, and identity on the inside of us so we can get up and fulfill it.

In John 11, Jesus is on His way to speak resurrection life to His friend Lazarus, and He runs into Martha. Martha tells Jesus that if He had been there, her brother would not have died. Jesus proceeded to tell Martha that her brother will rise again. Martha replied to Jesus that she knew he would rise again in the last day. But, then, Jesus made a statement in verse 25 that shocked Martha and the world: *"I am the Resurrection and the Life; he that believes in me, though he were dead, yet shall he live. And whoever lives and believes in me shall never die."* He asked Martha if she believed and she said yes, that she believed He was the Christ, the Son of God that came into the world. What is so amazing about this is that the word "resurrection" means "a standing up again to bring recovery."[33] So, when Jesus resurrected from the dead, He became the "stand up" and "recovery" of our life!

Going back to Ezekiel 37, Ezekiel is a type of Jesus to the children of Israel, in the middle of their captivity. He is used by God to bring formation and reformation back to the people of God through the power of prophecy. He prophesies the stand up and the recovery of Israel's life. Remember that prophecy is the spirit of affirmation and it comes to heal, nourish, and nurture, and it also comes to build up, stir up, and cheer up. The faith, or bones, of a nation responded to God's prophetic voice in the earth, as did the winds of the four corners. The Spirit of God is what brought resurrection power in that dry valley, but it took an Ezekiel, a man of God who carried a prophetic voice, whose name means strength, healing, and recovery, to prophecy to that dry, tight place. And, when he did, a great army stood up and this great army was none other than the house of God!

Regardless of whatever tight place you are going through, know that He is the God of your tight place. Rest assured that He will bring you to your resurrected place, because He is the stand up and the recovery of your life. If you find yourself in a dry tight place, remember to lift up your voice and prophesy strength, healing, and recovery and you, too, will see that He will bring you through!

As we move on to the next chapter, we will discover the power of increase as we journey together from a tight place to a wealthy place.

CHAPTER 8 – POWER POINTS

- There is power in your voice!
- Prophecy is expressing the heart of God and it is the spirit of affirmation.
- Prophesy strength, healing, and recovery and watch your solution stand up!

---

33 Strong, James. "Resurrection," Greek 386. *Strong's Exhaustive Concordance of the Bible.* Iowa Falls, Iowa: World Bible Publishers, 1986.

CHAPTER 9

THE POWER OF INCREASE
FROM A TIGHT PLACE TO A WEALTHY PLACE

In the preceding chapters, we have seen the faithfulness of our God, delivering and setting free through His power that works in us mightily. If you feel stuck or trapped in a tight place, know that God has a way of escape for you.

In this chapter, I want to take you from a tight place to a wealthy place by grasping the revelation of increase through Peter's journey of ups & downs and ins & outs. My intention is to help educate and relocate your faith in God, and to help mature the faith you already possess. My heart is to give you godly tools to help you navigate the twists and turns of life that can be so tremendously stressful and devastating.

ALL REVELATION HAS AN UNTIL MOMENT

If I were to ask you, "Which man is higher? The man painting the ceiling, or the man laying the carpet?", you would hopefully answer that it's the man painting the ceiling. But, what if you realized that the man laying the carpet was on the second floor? Or, if I was to ask you, "What's greater, 50 or 10?", you would hopefully say "50." But, that would only be until you realized that $10 is greater than 50 cents! My point is that all revelation has an "until" moment, a moment when a new response or perspective becomes clear. Every moment has a season of preparation connected to it for your season of opportunity. Anytime your preparation meets opportunity, it gives birth to the favor of God which is God's wealthy place.

When I was nine years old, my parents would let me go fishing by myself at the I-90 bridge in my hometown of Moses Lake, Washington. One day, I met a man named Eddie, who was amazing at catching crappie. This particular day he was putting on a fishing clinic, catching two crappies at a time! This was making everybody, including me, pretty jealous! Everyone wanted to know what he was using to be so successful and I finally worked up the nerve to ask him. He proceeded to tell me his little secret – it was a red and white mini jig tipped with a maggot! Before long, with this secret, it was not long until I was catching some fish, too. Needless to say, Eddie became my good fishing buddy that day because he taught me a new way to fish. However, he also did something that no one understood, including me. This was back in 1978, when afro hairstyles were in, and Eddie had two popsicle sticks that he had taped together to measure about 12 inches. He kept it stuck in his hair, so I thought it was his pick, but every time he caught a crappie, he would take those sticks out and measure the fish. If it was bigger than the stick, he would throw it back into the lake. After watching him do that a few times, I asked him what in the world he was doing, thinking it must be another secret trick. His response back to me? "Because, Joey, I only own a 12" pan!" I replied, "So, get a bigger pan!" Can I tell you that Eddie had an "until" moment?

I tell this story because, so often, people do not realize that God is wanting to bless them with what I call a "big fish" anointing, but they "throw the blessing back" just like Eddie, because they have a 12" mentality! We must fully come to understand that God's intention is to bless your socks off in every way at all times, for every good work. We must have a mindset shift so that we can obtain and sustain the blessing of the Lord.

MOVING FROM FAITH TO FAITH

Romans 1:16-17 says, *"I am not ashamed of the gospel of Christ, for it is the power of God to salvation for everyone who believes, for the Jew first and also for the Greek. For in it the righteousness of God is revealed from faith to faith; as it is written, 'The just shall live by faith.'"* As we journey in life, we realize how much faith is a vital part of our everyday life. How we believe and what we believe is crucial. We know, according to Hebrews 11:1, that, *"Faith is the substance of things hoped for and the evidence of things not seen."* I like to say it like this: Faith does not know *what* a thing is, as much as it knows *that* a thing is!

In Chapter 6, I touched on beginning faith and finishing faith. Remember that beginning faith is having faith to get saved, having faith to get baptized, having faith to get healed, and having faith to prosper. Finishing faith is faith to get people saved, get people baptized, get people healed, and the faith to see people prosper. One is for you and the other is for everybody else! When we can understand that God has put us on this earth to be a blessing by exercising our faith, we will move in the power of increase, taking us from our tight place to our wealthy place.

Let's look at the life of Peter as he progresses from faith to faith to move him from his tight place to his wealthy place.

THE POWER OF MENDING NETS

"And Jesus, walking by the Sea of Galilee, saw two brothers, Simon called Peter, and Andrew his brother, casting a net into the sea; for they were fishermen. Then He said to them, 'Follow Me, and I will make you fishers of men.' They immediately left their nets and followed Him. Going on from there, He saw two other brothers, James the son of Zebedee, and John his brother, in the boat with Zebedee their father, mending their nets. He called them, and immediately they left the boat and their father, and followed Him."

Matthew 4:18-22

When Jesus called Peter and Andrew, and said, "Follow Me," notice that they were casting a net into the sea because they were fishermen. When Jesus called James and John, they were in the boat with their dad, mending nets. Let me expound on the importance of having a seasoned father in the boat. A seasoned father who is a fisherman knows the times and seasons of when fish are schooling and when they are not schooling. They know the barometric pressure, the temperature of the water, the importance of high tide verses low tide, etc. They know where to go when it's hot and where to go when it's cold. Peter and Andrew are busy fishing by casting a net, and James and John are mending nets with their father in the boat. You see, when the fish are not schooling, you should be preparing or mending your nets (plural), not fishing with *a* net. Peter and Andrew only had one usable net because they were too busy fishing, when, on the other hand, Zebedee, the father of James and John, had his boys mending because it was not the time for fishing.

If you are going to move from a tight place to a wealthy place by the power of increase, you will have to understand the significance of preparation. To me, preparation is focusing on the main thing. Too often, we can get distracted by our own selfish desires, concerns, or worries. I have learned that distraction is the breeding ground for deception. Focus is the breeding ground for reception. One is a receiver, the other is a taker. In Luke 10:41, Jesus rebukes Martha because she's distracted and worried about many things. Hebrews 12:2 says, *"Looking away to all that would distract, looking unto Jesus the author and finisher of our faith."*

PREPARED VS. UNPREPARED

Let's consider Luke 5:1-9 to give us a better picture of what I am saying. The story goes like this: Jesus was preaching on Peter's boat after Peter had gone fishing and had caught nothing all day. When Jesus got done with His teaching, He looked at Peter and told him to let down his nets (notice that nets is plural). Peter replied, "Master, we have toiled all night and have caught nothing, but nevertheless, at your Word I will let down the net."

First of all, I want to remind you that Jesus is not afraid of your tight place of nothing and disappointment. We covered this, remember? He will confront your disappointment with the Word that He is! Secondly, Peter responded by putting down one net, but Jesus never said "put down your net," Jesus said put down your *nets* – that means more than one! But, because Peter was always busy fishing, he never had time to mend, so now he was unprepared for the big blessing!

The story proceeds with Peter dropping his net down and catching a great multitude of fish, and the Bible says that "their net broke." Their net broke because they were unprepared – when they should have been mending, they were fishing. We must have faith for the increase of blessing, but we also must have faith for preparation. When preparation meets opportunity, it gives birth to the favor of God.

The story goes on to say that when Peter saw the great multitude of fish and his net breaking, he waved down James and John to help them with the catch and both boats began to sink with the blessing by the power of increase. It is so important in your prophetic journey who you are connecting and partnering with – when you are not prepared for the blessing, at least the people you are connected to might be, simply because they had a father in the boat to teach and instruct them so they would not miss out on the blessing!

The last point I want you to look at with me is that the lake was called Gennesaret, which Easton's Bible Dictionary defines as "a garden of riches."[34] That's a wealthy place! The first time Peter went fishing in a "wealthy place," he caught nothing. If you are fishing in a wealthy place, then it's impossible to catch nothing – you must catch something! So, Jesus confronted Peter's tight place of disappointment, taking him back to the exact place where he was disappointed and showing him that all things are possible if you will just believe (see Mark 9:23). The rest is history for Peter – even though he was a little unprepared, God could still bring the power of increase to him because of who he was connected to. James and John were prepared because of a father in a boat giving them wisdom. It moved Peter from a tight and troubled place of disappointment after disappointment into a significant and beautiful wealthy place!

GROWING IN FAITH

In Ecclesiastes 9:11-12, the Bible tells us that the race is not to the swift, or the strong, or the wise. It's not even for those who are very skilled. It's for those who understand their "now time." This portion of Scripture is profound because here in this text, the word for "time" is translated "now time."[35] So, when you understand that it is your now time as a child of God, your faith will begin to grow exponentially. The enemy wants to keep you blinded in ignorance so that you never come to know your true identity as a child of God. All revelation has an "until" moment, and when you embrace that moment, then and only then will you discover that this race is not for the swift, nor

---

34 Easton, Matthew George. https://www.biblestudytools.com/dictionaries/eastons-bible-dictionary/gennesaret.html. Easton's Bible Dictionary. (Accessed March 2019).

35 Strong, James. "Time," Hebrew 6526. *Strong's Exhaustive Concordance of the Bible*. Iowa Falls, Iowa: World Bible Publishers, 1986.

the strong, and it's not even for the wise and the skilled, but for those who understand it's their NOW time!

Life has a way of throwing twists and turns at you, so that one moment you're up, the next moment you're down, another moment you're in, and another moment you're out. Peter's journey had some tough bumps along the way, but at the end, he recaptured his identity, and became the apostle of faith in the New Testament. Let's conclude with Peter's story in John 21 after the disciples saw Jesus crucified on the cross, and Peter decided to go fishing again.

GONE FISHING, AGAIN!

In John 21:3-11, Peter had just denied Jesus (as Jesus foretold), Judas had hung himself, and Jesus had been hung on the cross. They had all found out that Jesus had risen from the dead, and Peter was feeling horrible and lost, full of guilt and shame. He did not know what to do or where to go, so he decided to go back to doing what he used to do before Jesus called him to be a follower and a disciple. He went back to fishing!

After His resurrection, Jesus found them and asked them if they had caught any fish and they answered "no." Then, He told them to cast their net on the right side of the ship, and they would find some. Then, they caught a multitude of great fishes! In Luke 5, they caught a great multitude of fishes (that would mean a lot of little fish), but in John 21, they caught a multitude of great fishes. In fact, they caught 153 fish, which is symbolic of several things. For example, Jesus preached in exactly 153 cities, and there were 153 species of fish in the lake called Tiberias, which is another name for Gennesaret. The number 153 in the Hebrew gematria, which is a method of interpreting Scripture by assigning a number to a word based on its letters, and where numbers and letters are interchangeable, means "I am Elohim."[36] Wow!

Peter and the men caught more than just fish. In their tight place of feeling insignificant, lost, and ashamed, they caught back their identity that they had lost in the middle of their journey. Peter learned that he didn't have to be a slave to his past mistakes, but that he could repent and move forward into what God had for him.

---

36 Gematrix.org. https://www.gematrix.org/?word=153. (Accessed October, 2019).

God moves us from faith to faith, from preparation to preparation, and even from opportunity to opportunity. Sometimes, we don't foresee all the twist and the turns. But, one thing I know is that God's love for us is strong. Peter's prophetic journey shows us that God never gave up on him, through his good and bad, and loved him where he was. That, my friends, is how powerful Jesus' love is for us. It never gives up on us. Jesus is so faithful to see us through our dark and tough tight places. His love compels us to move onward and upward into His purposes and plans and breaks off any spirits of condemnation, guilt, or shame that would keep us bound, like Peter, to the past.

You can come through every tight place, by understanding your "until" moment that will bring a season of preparation for your day of opportunity and ultimately bring you to God's wealthy place.

LAST IMPRESSION

When you encounter your "until" moment and seize your season of preparation, you must hang on until opportunity comes then it will usher you in to your wealthy place. Once there, you will have to have a mindset shift in order for you to maintain and sustain the wealthy place. In Luke 10:30-37, Jesus tells the parable of the Good Samaritan, and in that story, we see contrasting mindsets.

The first mindset is that of the robber or the thief, and that mentality says, "What is yours is mine." The second mindset is of the priest and the Levite. I call this belief system a religious spirit, because that mentality says, "What is mine is mine." It was against their religion to touch dead people, so rather than contaminate themselves with the mess of the man they chose to hold their peace. The third mindset in the story is of the Good Samaritan, which says, "What is mine is yours. If I have it and it is within my means to help you, then what is mine is yours."

I believe there is an even better mindset than that of the Good Samaritan, however, and that is the mindset of God, which says, "What is God's is God's." To illustrate this point to my congregation one Sunday morning, I gave a $100 bill to one of my pastors before the service started. I told him that at a certain point in the sermon, I would ask for $100 and he should give it to me when I asked for it. He agreed, so when I was breaking down all these belief systems from this parable, I got to the last one and I said to my congregation, "It's my wife's birthday today and I would love to take her to a nice dinner tonight. Does anyone have a $100 bill that I could have to bless my wife?" You could feel the room tighten up just a little, but that was my cue for my pastor to come up and give me the $100 bill I had given him before service. I was so glad he remembered! People clapped their hands and other people wanted to come up and bless my wife, but I stopped everybody and made my point, which is that when you know that everything you have and everything you own belongs to the One Who created you, you don't have a problem giving it back to God. So, if He wants it, I should not have a problem giving to the One Who gave it to me – which is no different than my pastor giving me the $100 bill when I asked for it. It was easy for him to give me the $100 bill because it wasn't his, it was mine.

If we are going to be a people that will move from a tight place to a wealthy place and maintain that place, we will have to have a mindset shift that says, "What is God's is God's!" When we embrace that mindset, we will move from faith to faith, preparation to preparation, and opportunity to opportunity, and that will bring us to one wealthy place after another!

As we approach our final chapter of this book, my goal is to bring us from all of our tight places into a corporate place defined by the power of unity that will catapult us into the glory of God.

CHAPTER 9 – POWER POINTS

- We must expand our capacity so that we can be the recipients of God's blessing in our life.
- Focus is the breeding ground for reception. Distraction is the breeding ground for deception.
- The goal is to recognize our now moment!

CHAPTER 10

THE POWER OF UNITY
FROM A TIGHT PLACE TO A CORPORATE PLACE

As we have journeyed from our tight places to all of our promised places, we have learned that God is faithful to His word and to His people. From every heartbreak and dilemma, to every confrontation of barrenness and giants, God was the ultimate faith factor. We saw God affirm patriarchs in the middle of their weakness, giving them the ability to confront obstacles and impossibilities that were standing in their way. We also witnessed the incredible patience of a loving God toward a rebellious prophet who discovered very quickly you cannot curse what God has already blessed. We saw the greatness and the faithfulness of our God in the life of Peter as he journeyed through insecurities and inferiorities in his life. In the previous chapter, we learned that God has some wealthy places for us to possess and maintain, and that as we move from faith to faith, we will begin to mature into the sons and daughters of God that He has called us to be. Encountering the power of increase will catapult us from a lot of little things to a great deal of big things!

In this final chapter, my heart is to bring understanding to you about the power of unity and shine a light on the dynamic power of the Spirit of God when the corporate body comes together. When the Body of Christ begins to assemble, with Jesus as the head, power is released. So, come with me as I unfold the mystery of the corporate anointing that will thrust you into your prophetic journey, from your tight place to your corporate place of belonging.

THE POWER OF ORDER

There's an important progression in 1 Corinthians 10-14. In order to commune with God effectively, we must read 1 Corinthians 10, which talks about order or position. When you get in proper position or order, your position will start changing your condition. Your position will allow you to commune with God and His people, which leads into the communion covered in 1 Corinthians 11. Communion is not just vertical, between you and God. It starts there, but communion is also horizontal. You must learn to commune with God's people and that's what is sometimes so difficult. From there, Chapter 12 is about unity, and unity is the power of the Kingdom of God. Chapter 13 is about love, where you realize you can't fail. The whole chapter of 1 Corinthians 14, then, deals with the administration and the release of the Holy Spirit.

If we become a people unified by the Holy Spirit, then we will easily grasp the power of God's love, in which nothing can fail. With that revelation, you can't help but be a blessing to everyone you know who needs a touch or a word from Him, by releasing the power of the Holy Spirit!

THE POWER OF UNITY

Unity is the power of the Kingdom. The word "power" is in the Strong's Concordance as the word "dunamis," which means "God's strength, power, and ability."[37] In the New American Standard New Testament Greek Lexicon, "dunamis" is derived as "moral power" and "movement power," as well as "money power," "multiplication power," and "miracle power."[38] So, God gives us the ability and power to live morally righteous. Then, He gives us the strength and ability to move things in and out of our lives. That's why we can say to whatever mountain we're facing to get out of the way and be thrown into the sea, not doubting in our heart, but believing that what we say will come to pass (see Mark 11:23). It is God Who gives us the power to get wealth (according to Deuteronomy 8:18), so He can establish His covenant on the earth. He wants to give us money power to do things for advancing the Kingdom of God. He wants to give us multiplication power and miracle power

37 Strong, James. "Power," Greek 1411. *Strong's Exhaustive Concordance of the Bible*. Iowa Falls, Iowa: World Bible Publishers, 1986.

38 Thayer and Smith. "Dunamis." *The NAS New Testament Greek Lexicon*. https://www. biblestudytools.com/lexicons/greek/nas/dunamis.html. 1999. (Accessed March 2019).

so we can do the supernatural, like feeding the multitudes, as Jesus did with the loaves and the fish (see Matthew 14:13-21).

When I was in South Africa in 2007, I was doing a large crusade for a township to help a few of the pastors there in Johannesburg. We were told that about 400 people would fill the gymnasium. Well, there was about 1,200 and counting, but we had only brought enough food for 400 people. I gathered my team and said, "If Jesus can do it, so can we." Through the power of agreement and unity, I began to pray, and what happened next was beyond incredible. We not only fed 1,200 people, but we still had half a trailer full of food! I am telling you that if you could unite with some believers, you could do some incredible things through the power of unity.

WHAT'S ON THE HEAD COMES ON THE BODY

"Behold, how good and how pleasant it is for brethren to dwell together in unity! It is like the precious oil upon the head, running down on the beard, the beard of Aaron, running down on the edge of his garments. It is like the dew of Hermon, descending upon the mountains of Zion; for there the Lord commanded the blessing – life forevermore."

Psalm 133:1-5

In this passage, we see a prevailing principle laid out for us that is so profound when understood properly. It is the principle that whatever is on the head comes on the body. Now, if that is true, and it is, then the principle of reversal is, as well. Whenever the body comes together, the head is present. With this understanding, let's look further in detail about the revelation of the body coming together.

In 1 Corinthians 12:12, we discover that we are the Body of Christ, and members in particular, and in Colossians 1:18, we see that Jesus is the head of that body called Christ. So, knowing through Scripture that Jesus is the head and we are His body, we must understand now the power that the head brings to the body. In Scripture, every time the Body assembles in unity, Jesus can't help but be the head of that Body.

Let's take a look at some examples. In Acts 2, Jesus tells the disciples to wait in Jerusalem until they are clothed with power ("dunamis") from on high.

The chapter goes on to say, *"When the Day of Pentecost had fully come, they were all with one accord in one place. And suddenly there came a sound from heaven, as of a rushing mighty wind, and it filled the whole house where they were sitting."* The third person of the Godhead could not come down until there was a people assembled who understood the power of unity. The sad part is that Jesus told over 500 people to wait in Jerusalem, but only 120 endured with patience and long-suffering.

Another story is found in the book of Acts again, in Acts 16:25-32. Here, we have the story of Paul and Silas being put in prison because Paul cast some demons out of a little girl who was a fortuneteller. That really upset her owner, who created quite the stir in the city, and both Paul and Silas were thrown into prison. But, at midnight, they began to sing songs of worship, and Jesus couldn't help but be the head of that body in unity, and the power to set them free was released.

This power is also found in Daniel 3:16-25, where we have three Hebrew boys named Shadrach, Meshach, and Abednego, who refused to bow to King Nebuchadnezzar's golden image. This was reported to the king, who asked them why they did not bow to his god, and the boys said that they worship the one true God, the God of Israel. So, the king proceeded to tell the three Hebrew boys that if they did not bow, they would be thrown into the fiery furnace. The boys all responded in unity, "We will not bow!" This made the king even angrier, and he ordered the fire to be made seven times hotter. After they threw them in, King Nebuchadnezzar looked into the fiery furnace and was astonished! He asked his counselors, "Didn't we throw in three Hebrew boys?" They replied yes, but the king responded that he saw four people in the fiery furnace, walking unharmed in the midst of the fire, and the fourth was like the Son of God!

Anytime that we responsibly make up the body of Christ, Jesus can't help but be the head of that body, and anytime He becomes the head of the Body, power is released. I am reminded of pointer dogs, which are used for hunting pheasants and other kinds of birds. When one of these dogs smells a bird, that dog goes "on-point" in the direction that of the bird. When the other dogs see that the dog is on-point, they all automatically go on-point, too. They call that "honoring the point." So, if these hunting dogs get it, why can't we get it? When somebody in the Church is sensing God's presence and is either clapping, crying, or leaping, why can't we "honor the point?" I believe this is part of us mastering the spirit of unity. The power of the corporate anointing will thrust us into the glorious victories designed for us as the people of God.

THE DESIRES OF YOUR HEART

Psalms 37:4-5 reads, *"Delight yourself also in the Lord, and He shall give you the desires of your heart. Commit your way to the Lord, trust also in Him, and He shall bring it to pass."* Here we see another prevailing principle laid out in the Word of God. First of all, we have the word "delight," then we have the word "desire." When we delight ourselves in the Lord, He puts desires on the inside of us. And, when we commit our way to the Lord, and trust also in Him, notice that He is the One responsible for bringing it to pass. Our job is easy! We delight, commit, and trust, and He will bring it to pass. This principle states that if I do my part, God will do His part. If I am doing my job, delighting, committing, and trusting, and I don't see my desire outside of me, it is because God has put the desire on the inside of me. So, the governing principle according to Ecclesiastes 3:11 says, *"He hath made everything beautiful in his time: also, he hath set eternity in their heart."* Everything that is beautiful lies in the womb of darkness. For a butterfly to become beautiful, it has to go through a metamorphosis, a transformation, into a deep sleep that feels like death itself. But, when the process is finished, out comes that caterpillar from the cocoon, ushering in newness of life. With this knowledge, let's proceed with the three stories below.

DEEP SLEEP #1

In 1 Samuel 26:12, we find King Saul wasting all his time and effort trying to kill David because he knows that God has put His hand on him to be king over Israel. God puts King Saul and his men in a deep sleep. The word for "deep sleep" comes from the root word "radam" which means "put to death."[39] This paints the picture that God killed them. God dealt with Saul and his army, but God tested David in this situation to see what he would do. David did not

---

39 Strong, James. "Radam," Hebrew 7290. *Strong's Exhaustive Concordance of the Bible.* Iowa Falls, Iowa: World Bible Publishers, 1986.

kill King Saul, because David feared God more than he feared the king, and David knew he couldn't touch God's anointed. So, David took the spear that had been thrown at him three times, and the jug of water, then woke them up. King Saul knew at that moment that something had shifted. David knew that if he preserved the king, then the King of Kings would preserve him from all his tight places. David knew that if God killed them, then he didn't have to, and that day, everybody there knew that God had given David the throne.

DEEP SLEEP #2

Genesis 15:12-18 records the story of a deep sleep falling upon Abram and God speaking to him about his descendants and a period of slavery. God told him that he would be buried in peace, but that affliction would come to other generations. God wanted to make a covenant with Abram, but didn't want him to mess things up. So, God put Abram in a deep sleep, because Abram's desire was not on the outside of him, but on the inside of him. So, God came down from heaven like a smoking furnace and a burning torch, to make a covenant with Himself, and for Himself.

The Bible says in Hebrews 6:13, *"When God made a promise to Abraham, because He could swear by no one greater, He swore by Himself, saying, 'Surely, in blessing I will bless you, and in multiplying I will multiply you.'"* God made a covenant with Abram, so He could give him his name and turn him from Abram to Abraham. God became his father and Abraham became His son forever. God made a promise to Abraham and his seed, called Christ, so that if you belong to Christ, then you are Abraham's seed, and heirs according to that promise (see Galatians 3:29). Abraham was put in a deep sleep to receive the covenant of Almighty God.

DEEP SLEEP #3

In Genesis 2:21-24, we see the account of God causing Adam to fall into a deep sleep so God could take one of his ribs to fashion Eve. Adam had been naming all the animals of the field, and when he was done he realized that he was the only one who looked like his kind. This is when God said it was not good for man to be alone. I believe that Adam was craving relationship and love, and looking for a potential mate. Anytime you're delighting yourself in the Lord, and committing your way unto Him, He puts desire in you. So, Adam was doing the right things and God put this desire on the inside of him. When you are craving something and you don't find it outside of you, it is because God has hidden it on the inside of you. That was the case with Adam, so in order for God to get it out of him, He had to put Adam to sleep. As God did this, He built Adam a wife and companion who was bone of his bone and flesh of his flesh. The Bible goes on to says in verse 24 that, *"For this reason, a man shall leave his father and mother, to cleave to his wife that the two would become one flesh."*

NOWHERE TO LAY HIS HEAD

Matthew 8:20 says, *"And Jesus said to him, 'Foxes have holes and birds of the air have nests, but the Son of Man has nowhere to lay His head.'"* This is not referring to Jesus having nowhere to sleep, but that Jesus doesn't have a mature body to rest His headship on, so that there could be reproduction. You see, foxes don't live in holes, they reproduce in holes, and birds of the air don't live in nests, they reproduce in nests. The word "lay" in this text is the same Greek word for "bowing" in John 19:30, which says, *"So, when Jesus had received the sour wine, He said, 'It is finished!' And bowing His head, He gave up His spirit."*[40]

At the cross, Jesus, for the first time in human history, found a place to lay His head. Just like the first Adam, Jesus delighted in the Lord and committed His way to Him, so the Father put Jesus' desire on the inside of Him. When Jesus arrived at the Jordan and was baptized, He came into His Sonship and began to look for His mate, so that He could reproduce. But, when Jesus began to look outside of Himself for what He desired, all he saw was a Pharisaical system that was beautiful on the outside, but full of dead man's bones on the inside. Jesus thought, "That's not my wife." When He looked again, He saw a Sadducaical system that looked good on the outside, but had no resurrection power and again He said, "That's not my wife, either."

So, when you can't find the desires of what you're looking for on the outside, it's because it's on the inside of you. The Father had to put Jesus in a deep sleep to get out what He was looking for, which was His bride, the Church of the living God, who is bone of His bone.

---

40 Strong, James. "Bowed," Greek 2827. *Strong's Exhaustive Concordance of the Bible.* Iowa Falls, Iowa: World Bible Publishers, 1986.

Now John 19:25-30 makes even more sense. Jesus looked at his mother Mary, and said, *"Woman, behold your son, and son, behold your mother."* Jesus, at the cross, found His bride and His Church. It was on the inside of Him the whole time. He was the only one of the God-kind in the earth, but He had finally found His bride, called the Church. Basically, what He was saying to John and Mary was, "I found her, and for this reason a man shall leave his father and mother to cleave with his spouse." Wow!

The cross was the marriage of Jesus and His Church. Just like Adam, when Jesus Christ was put to sleep, He got the woman of His dreams, and just like Adam, He discovered her not on the outside of Himself, but on the inside of Himself – the glorious Church, full of power and might. Just like Abraham, who was put into a deep sleep to get the covenant, Jesus was put to sleep to give every man and every woman a new and better covenant. Just like King David, who released forgiveness on the man who wanted to kill him, Jesus released mercy. Mercy triumphs over judgment every time, and because of the power of pardon, King David inherited the throne of mercy. So, our heavenly King Jesus, the son of David, would be hung on an old rugged cross to utter out of His righteous lips, in Luke 23:34, "Father, forgive them for they know not what they do." When the King of all kings forgave the whole world, Jesus Christ inherited the throne of grace forever and ever, and to whosoever who will believe in His name, Jesus the Son of God will extend the throne of His great grace.

If the Church could ever get the revelation of the corporate anointing, we would move in greater dimensions of authority and power! It would catapult us from our tight places to our corporate place of unity where we would experience the transformation of a loving God!

CHAPTER 10 – POWER POINTS

• Unity is the power of the Kingdom.
• Every time the Body assembles in unity, Jesus can't help but be the head of that Body, and then power is released.
• Jesus has found His bride, the Church, and provided a greater covenant with us – with the revelation of unity, we can operate in authority and power!

CONCLUSION

My intention in writing this book was to take you on a prophetic journey through the lives of many notable and familiar Bible characters, who were people just like us, with all kinds of problems and dysfunctions. But, God still saw them through from one tight place after another tight place, and brought them through every time. My heart is to charge you, challenge you, and hope that God would change you by understanding that in your prophetic journey, He is the God of all your tight places.